93-957

Emigrants to America

Indentured Servants
Recruited in London
1718-1733

EMIGRANTS TO AMERICA

Indentured Servants Recruited in London 1718-1733

JOHN WAREING

Principal Lecturer in Geography,
The Polytechnic of North London

GENEALOGICAL PUBLISHING CO., INC.
Baltimore 1985

ACKNOWLEDGEMENT

Thanks are due to the Corporation of London for permission
to publish for the first time the edited register of indentured servants for the period 1718-1733.

PART ONE

THE BINDING OF
INDENTURED SERVANTS IN LONDON

Part One:

THE BINDING OF
INDENTURED SERVANTS IN LONDON

The distinction that has been made between a free, European flow of transatlantic migrants and a forced, African flow has a general validity, but as was well demonstrated by A. E. Smith in his study of white servitude and convict labor in America, this distinction must be substantially qualified, at least during the colonial period.[1] Not all Europeans who crossed the Atlantic before 1776 were free men, and significant numbers of convicts, rogues and vagabonds, and political and military prisoners were transported into involuntary servitude. Most important of all were the indentured servants who entered voluntary servitude but whose status as free men, at least in the short term, is rather ambiguous.[2]

Smith took the view that indentured servants were transported from the British Isles as human cargo in a trade in which they played a predominantly passive role, with the real stimulus coming from the activities of recruiting agents. A recent study has challenged this view and has suggested that the indenture was the outcome of a process of bargaining between the prospective servant and a recruiter competing with other merchants for the servant's business.[3] However, the amount of freedom of choice that this implies raises problems, and there is clear evidence to show that many indentured servants played very little part in their migration decision.

Whatever the truth of the matter, and this writer believes that it is not possible to generalize for all servants for the whole colonial period in this way since circumstances changed substantially from the seventeenth to the eighteenth century, the importance of indentured servitude as an institution of vital importance in the peopling of Britain's American colonies has not been challenged.

The System of Indentured Servitude

Indentured servitude played a central role in the peopling of the American colonies, and between one-half and two-thirds of all persons who went to the colonies south of New England were servants, forming the backbone of the whole migratory movement. Equally important, servants formed the principal supply of labor until well into the eighteenth century in the mainland colonies.[4]

It was a system under which white people, who were unable or unwilling to pay the costs of passage, became bond servants to a colonial master for a period of years, usually via a third party or agent who arranged their passage. This principle of bond service was not new and was well established in England in the form of apprenticeship or the hiring of farm servants. The practice was suggested for colonial settlement as early as 1582, was working in Virginia in 1619, and by 1636 was well-enough established for printed forms to be in use. It lasted as a method of emigration from Britain until 1785, in which year the transport of persons on English vessels for the purposes of debt was prohibited.[5]

If those immigrants taken under involuntary servitude are excluded, and convicts constituted no more than 20 per cent of European immigrants to the mainland colonies, there were three methods by which servants were taken to Britain's American colonies. This work is concerned with the operation of the first of these whereby the servant left for the colonies with an indenture, or legal contract. This indenture bound the servant to give, usually, four year's service to whichever colonial master bought it from the transporting agent upon the servant's arrival in the colony. In return, the servant received passage, keep, and perhaps a specified reward at the end of the period of service. Such indentures were of a generally standard form during any one period, but they could be amended at the time of binding to the advantage of either the servant or the agent through variations in the length of service or the inclusion of special conditions.[6] Voluntary servitude was thus a temporary status somewhere between freedom and slavery, and upon arrival in a colonial port the servant was displayed on the deck of the ship and sold to the highest bidder.

There was a variation in this practice whereby a servant was not sold immediately upon arrival but was allowed, as was John Watson of Yorkshire, "ten days next after his arrival to seek his redemption" in May 1683. A further two such "redemptioners" can be identified later in the same year who were to have ten days and one week respectively to find their passage money and thus avoid servitude.[7] This second method of taking servants to the colonies, in which the intending migrant would pay part of the passage money to an agent and be given a certain amount of time to find the balance upon arrival is usually described as an eighteenth-century practice, but the essential elements were clearly established much earlier. However, in its modified form, this method increased in importance after 1700, and many more redemptioners than indentured servants were carried across the Atlantic in the eighteenth century. In the event, most redemptioners were unable to raise the balance in the fourteen days commonly allowed and thus became indentured servants with the length of service dependent upon the size of the debt, but the eighteenth-century redemptioners, usually family groups from Europe, constitute a different category of migrant from individual servants from the British Isles bound before departure.[8]

Substantial numbers, and probably a majority, of servants reached the colonies by a third method. They went without an indenture and relied upon "the custom of the country" to get indenture terms when they arrived according to the laws established by colonial governments in line with local practices. Some of these servants may have been kidnap victims, many more were part of mass migrations or special schemes, and others were recruited by the friends, families, or agents of colonists in the manner that Moll Flanders used her former governess to obtain three women servants or that Colonel Jack had the services of a permanent correspondent in London to obtain the things that he wanted.[9]

The Role of the Emigration Agent

The driving force behind the migration of indentured servants was a continuing strong demand for labor in the colonies, which was later translated into a demand for white men in the Caribbean colonies.[10] To this can be added, at least by the eighteenth century, the pull of opportunities that colonial conditions offered to the migrant. On the supply side there is little doubt that there existed in London a considerable pool of labor resulting from the large-scale

10

migration to the city and whose very volume led to restricted opportunities for many aspirants.[11] Indeed, servitude has been described as a safety valve for London.[12] Moveover, the spirit of the age, despite Mercantilist opposition to emigration after 1660, promoted adventure, and, in addition, the colonies presented a convenient venue for the disposal of the unwanted.

However, although push-pull theories of migration are attractive because they are simple and common-sensical, the model implies friction, and this is not always easily overcome. It has been noted, for example, that the inability to go, because of a lack of means, was cause for comment right through the famine in nineteenth-century Ireland.[13] In the formulation of push-pull models insufficient attention has been paid to means, but the history of emigration from the British Isles contains many agents and agencies with a variety of motives and methods who have facilitated passage, and they were particularly active during the colonial period.

It is clear that the general economic role of the agents was to help colonial employers satisfy their demand for labor, and to enable servants in London to sell their labor in the high-wage colonial economies by providing the latter with the means of overcoming the problem of the considerable distance, however measured, between demand and supply. In so doing the agent was able to take up excess capacity in ships engaged in colonial trade and to make a tidy profit for himself.

What is less clear is the precise role that agents played in recruiting servants. A small proportion of indentured servants went to the colonies against their will as kidnap victims, and many more went willingly, but there was a substantial number of the young, gullible, impressionable, or ignorant somewhere in between where the distinction between persuasion, over-persuasion, and coercion is not clear.

It has been argued that because of the profits involved the servant trade was organized by and for the benefit of the emigration agents. In this trade, an agent, for an outlay of £4-10 on keep and passage, could get a return of £6-30 (with perhaps an additional bonus in the form of headrights), depending upon the state of the labor market of a particular colony and the quality of the servant. This "human cargo" model of the servant trade sees the agent as an enticing, inveigling procurer operating across the margins of legality, and can be contrasted with the "human capital" model of the trade in which the servant sold his skills through the agent in a rational market where the agent and servant negotiated as equals.[14]

Legislation and Data

There is little doubt that over-persuading and even kidnapping did take place. As a result of concern over kidnapping an ordinance of Parliament was enacted against the stealing of children in 1645, although there had been a prosecution for this offence at the Middlesex Sessions in 1643.[15] Despite this and other measures the number of prosecutions increased and the "spirits" thrived. The total number of kidnap victims is not likely to have been large, but it produced a hostile climate of opinion and there was a clear need for a system of registration to protect merchants from unfounded charges of kidnapping. A registry office was opened in 1664, but was not very effective, and it was not until a group of important Jamaica merchants petitioned the King and Council and obtained a new order in 1682 that a system was instituted which gave the merchants some protection against denunciation and dishonest servants.[16] However, the merchants wanted a system that would give them total protection against prosecution once a servant had been registered, but this was not granted until an Act of Parliament containing a clause to this effect was passed in 1717.[17]

These two pieces of legislation produced four types of records of indentured servants sailing from London. First, there are entries of agreements in the Lord Mayor's Waiting Books covering the period 1683-86 [889 servants]. Secondly, there are entries of registrations preserved in the records of the Fishmongers' Company almost certainly made during the 1680s [405 servants]. Thirdly, actual indenture forms used to bind individuals for service in the colonies survive for the periods 1683-86 [812 servants], 1718-25 [1,119 servants], 1727-39 [1,793 servants], and 1749-59 [263 servants]. Fourthly, a register of these indenture forms was drawn up for the period 1718-33 and includes the names of 1,544 servants for whom there is no surviving indenture and which have not previously been published.[18]

At their fullest these records give the name, age, place of origin, occupation, and signature or mark of a servant; his destination and period of service; the name, place of origin, and occupation of the agent to whom he was bound; and the name of the ship on which he was to travel and the name of her captain. Names of magistrates and witnesses might also be given, together with other miscellaneous information. However, it must be remembered that the records are not consistent. Very few give the whole range of data, and there is no way of knowing how complete or representative they are, especially in relation to the estimated 300,000-400,000 servants entering Britain's American colonies from all sources in the period 1650-1780.

NOTES

1. D. Eltis, "Free and Coerced Transatlantic Migrations: Some Comparisons," *American Historical Review* 88 [1983]: 251-80; Abbot E. Smith, *Colonists in Bondage: White Servitude and Convict Labor in America, 1607-1776* [Chapel Hill, 1947].

2. "They are more properly called slaves," writes Defoe in 1722 in *Moll Flanders.*

3. Smith, *op.cit.,* 39; D. Galenson, *White Servitude in Colonial America: An Economic Analysis* [Cambridge, 1981], 99.

4. Smith, *op. cit.,* 4, 25, 336.

5. R. B. Morris, *Government and Labor in Early America* [New York, 1946], 322.

6. Smith, *op. cit.,* 17.

7. John Wareing, "Some Early Emigrants to America, 1683-84: A Supplementary List," *Genealogists' Magazine* 18 [1976]: 242; C. D. P. Nicholson, "Some Early Emigrants to America," *Genealogists' Magazine* 12 [1955-58] and 13 [1959-60], indenture numbers 431 and 471.

8. Smith, *op. cit.,* 21-22; D. George, *London Life in the Eighteenth Century* [London, 1925], 144.

9. Daniel Defoe, *Moll Flanders* [1722] and *Colonel Jack* [1722]; Smith, *op. cit.,* 53.

10. Smith, *op. cit.,* 4, 30, 52.

11. John Wareing, "Migration to London and Transatlantic Emigration of Indentured Servants, 1683-1775," *Journal of Historical Geography* 7 [1981]: 356-78.

12. D. George, *op. cit.,* 148.

13. S. H. Cousins, "The Regional Pattern of Emigration During the Great Irish Famine, 1846-1851," *Transactions and Papers of the Institute of British Geographers* 28 [1960]: 128.

14. Smith, *op. cit.,* 86; Galenson, *op. cit.,* 99.

15. Peter W. Coldham, "The 'Spiriting' of London Children to Virginia, 1648-85," *Virginia Magazine of History and Biography* 83 [1975]: 280-87.

16. *CSP [Colonial]* 1681-85 [London, 1898], 317-18; *Acts of the Privy Council [Colonial]* 1680-Q1720 [London, 1910], 41-43.

17. The Act was 4 Geo I, c. 11. The clause is printed as Appendix to Part Two.

18. The first three sources are available in published form in:

   [A.] Entries of registrations in the Lord Mayor's Waiting Books: Michael Ghirelli, *A List of Emigrants from England to America 1682-1692* [Baltimore, 1968]; John Wareing, "The Emigration of Indentured Servants from London, 1683-86," *Genealogists' Magazine* 19 [1978].

   [B.] Entries of registrations preserved in the records of the Fishmongers' Company [almost certainly for the 1680s]: M. J. Chandler, "Emigrants from Britain to the Colonies of America and the West Indies," *Journal of the Barbados Museum and Historical Society* 36 [1979]: 28-43.

   [C.] Actual indenture forms: C. D. P. Nicholson, "Some Early Emigrants to America," *Genealogists' Magazine* 12 [1955-58] and 13 [1959-60]; John Wareing, "Some Early Emigrants to America: A Supplementary List, 1683-84," *Genealogists' Magazine* 18 [1976]; Jack and Marion Kaminkow, *A List of Emigrants from England to America 1718-1759* [Baltimore, 1964]; D. Galenson, "Agreements to Serve in America and the West Indies 1727-31," *Genealogists' Magazine* 19 [1977].

   [D.] A register of indentures in the City of London Record Office: Printed here as Part Three.

PART TWO

INTERPRETING THE REGISTER

PART TWO:

INTERPRETING THE REGISTER

In the Records Office of the Corporation of London there is a previously unpublished document numbered CLRO 204B and entitled

A register of the names and surnames of those persons who have voluntarily contracted and bound themselves to go beyond the Seas into His Majesties Colonies and Plantations in America and Certified to the Sessions according to the Statute in that case made and provided.

The statute referred to is the clause in the Act of Parliament passed in 1717, printed here as Appendix to Part Two. The Act was made to enable merchants legally to transport indentured servants to America for periods of up to eight years, providing that the servants were taken willingly before the Lord Mayor or some other Justice of the Peace if they were bound in the City of London. The servant would there sign the contract or indenture which would then be registered at the next Sessions. It can be seen that the Act was specifically concerned with the registration of minors between the ages of fifteen and twenty, but the register held in the Records Office also includes the names of adults. This can be established by comparing entries in the register with original indenture forms that have survived, and it is clear that many of the entries in the register for the period after 1722 are for adults. The adults were bound on a different type of form from that used for minors, and it appears that merchants were using the registration procedure whenever they could to protect themselves from accusations of illegally transporting people against their will.

The period covered by the register is from June 1718 to March 1733, but although there is a flourish at the end of the list on page 62, suggesting that the register ends, it is not possible to know how complete or accurate a record it gives of indentured servants bound in the City, except that it is certainly not comprehensive.

The register consists of sixty-seven sheets of paper bound in a parchment cover and measures approximately 7½" x 10" overall. Sixty-two pages of the register have been ruled in pencil on both sides and contain hand-written entries in ink of the names of approximately 3,398 indentured servants bound to serve in the English colonies in the West Indies and mainland North America. Also given are the names of ninety-five agents to whom they were bound, the colony to which they were destined, and either the date of the Sessions at which the indentures were certified or the actual date appearing on the indenture. A typical entry, located by date, would read: "John Abbett To Peter Simpson for Pensilvania." The actual number of entries in the register is 3,419, but because of the problem that some names are entered twice, a total of 3,190 men and 208 women is offered as a more accurate total of servants.

The purpose of the register is not entirely consistent, because although it may have been originally intended as a register of indentures made, as will be discussed below, it appears later to have become a record of indenture forms held by the Corporation, and it does not include all of those.

Original indenture forms certified in the City have survived for 1,854 of these servants and have been published together with details of a further 156 servants recruited in the period from 1718 to March 1733 who do not appear in the register but whose indenture forms have nevertheless survived. In fact, a note appears in the margin of the register for October 1724 that "some in this month left out but are in the bundle," and about two-thirds of these surviving indenture forms not included in the register are dated between November 1724 and March 1725. In addition, there are indenture forms surviving for a further 901 servants in the period from April 1733 to December 1739 immediately following the period covered by the register, and another 264 for the period from 1749 to 1759. It is not possible to know whether any further indenture forms have survived, although 65 turned up unexpectedly in the Court of Aldermen papers about 1970, but it appears unlikely.

All of this leaves 1,462 men and 82 women for whom there is no indenture surviving but whose names appear in the register together with other information presented in the lists below. These early Americans and the information concerning them are listed in Part Three, and the manner in which they have been abstracted and edited is discussed under the following five headings:

Dates

The register is primarily organized by date and covers the period from June 1718 to March 1733. However, two different sets of dates are used and a strict chronological sequence is not kept after 1730. The first set constitutes

21

the dates of the eight Sessions held each year at which the indenture could be registered. The second set constitutes the dates appearing on the actual indenture forms, given as month and year, and is used for the period after 1730.

Examination of the dates in the register can be used to investigate its history and purpose, and the register appears to fall into three parts. The first covers the period from 1718 to October 1724, is based on Sessions dates, and during the early part of this period the register was probably kept quite carefully. It is dated in the old style in accordance with the Julian Calendar, whereby, for example, December 1722 was followed by January 1722, and the year 1723 began on Lady Day, March 25. Even in this period the register is not complete since there are over twenty known indenture forms not included in it, nor is it entirely chronological since a group of servants who were certificated before Sir Thomas Abney between January 1721 and January 1722 were entered before those bound at the Sessions of July 1721. Moreover, by 1723 there are bindings recorded for only three of the Sessions held that year, and indentures dated as early as July 1723 are not recorded until January 1724.

The second part covers the period from October 1724 to December 1729 and begins with a handwriting change. It also is based on Sessions dates but contains a number of features which raise questions about the chronology used. The first of these is the fact that December 1724 is followed in the register by January 1725, and this practice is continued for entries until 1729, yet the new-style Gregorian Calendar which established January 1 as New Year's Day was not adopted in England until 1752. A second feature is that where comparisons are possible between entries and indenture forms, many of the forms are dated after the Sessions had been held. Unfortunately, it is not possible to compare any entries with indenture forms for the months of January to March during the period 1725 to 1729 in the section of the register where entries are made under Sessions headings, but there are entries for 1729 later in the register where it is clear that old-style dates have been entered in new-style sequence. Finally, at the point in the register where Sessions dates are replaced by dates taken from the indenture forms, the sequence of entries from the Sessions of December 2, 1729 to a surviving indenture for March 26, 1730 raises suspicions that entries for January 1 to March 24, 1729/30 have been made earlier in the register for the year 1729.

These suspicions are reinforced by entries in the third part of the register which covers the period from 1730 with some scattered entries for 1726 and 1729. Entries here are grouped by month and year from the dates on the indenture forms, and although they are not arranged in a strict chronology it is clear that old-style dates have been entered in new-style sequence.

On the basis of this evidence it appears that all the dates in the register are old-style dates, despite the arrangement of the Sessions headings for the period 1725-29 and the sequence of entries used after 1730. The following lists have been edited accordingly and the dates are presented new-style.

The conclusion is drawn that the register is an incomplete record of the bindings of indentured servants sworn in the period to May 1724 and written more or less at the time, but that for entries dated from October 1724 the register is a record, admittedly incomplete, of indenture forms held by the Corporation and was probably made later in the century at some time after 1752. The major effect of this, as will be discussed below, has been on the recording of destinations.

Servants

The above findings do not affect the accuracy of the genealogical information contained in the register where the names of the indentured servants who were carried across the Atlantic to the American and West Indian colonies are listed. There are 1,544 such names which have not previously been published and which are presented as Part Three. They are numbered and arranged in alphabetical order but are otherwise unedited and appear as they are written in the register.

It must be remembered that the names have been copied from original indenture forms and that there may be errors of transcription, but these are likely to be few. The principal problem is the well-known one that there was no standard spelling of surnames in the eighteenth century, and from the evidence of the surviving indenture forms which have been signed by the servants, the signatures on 17 per cent of the forms vary in spelling from the entry of the name made by the clerk. Moreover, 34 per cent of the indenture forms are signed with a mark, and it is clear that the name of an illiterate servant spelt phonetically by a clerk is likely to produce variations. As a result, we can hear the regional accents in names such as Cairstiers, O'Railey, and Gillburd, while others such as Pew, Goff, and Jakes may conceal alternative spellings.

It may be noted that women account for only 5.3 per cent of the servants included here, which reflects the fact that indentured servants were usually male.

Agents

Although the register gives a list of the names of servants bound to serve in the colonies, the names are arranged in groups associated with particular agents, and this reflects the fact, clearly indicated in the Act, that the system of registration was initiated for the benefit of the agents rather than for the servants.

The agent was responsible for persuading or obtaining the consent of the servant to be bound in the first place, for keeping him in London until his departure for the colonies, and for arranging his transport across the Atlantic. Once there, the servant would either be employed by a master who had used the agent to find someone for him in London with the skills that he needed, or, more usually, openly sold to an employer who was looking for workers.

In the register are the names of ninety-five agents who transported the 3,398 servants, and forty-eight of these are listed here for the 1,544 servants with no surviving indenture. [There are a further three agents who do not appear in the register but who have surviving indentures for the period.] Of course the forty-eight agents did not each transport the same number of servants, and over 84 per cent of the servants were transported by just eight agents, of whom John Taylor, James Gerald, and Peter Simpson were the most important. The emergence of large-scale operators such as these in London in this period marked a change from the way in which the business was operated in the period 1683-86 and for which there are similar data available. The average agent transported only three servants in the earlier period, but this had increased to thirty-three servants per agent in the period 1718-39.

Because of the nature of the system the information concerning the agents is likely to be very accurate, but there exists the problem of the variable spelling of surnames. In the lists the spelling of the names of the agents has been standardized.

Destinations

Perhaps the most difficult problem arises from the interpretation of the entries of destinations. For one or two entries no destination is recorded, for a few others more than one destination is given, but the major problem concerns the accuracy of the entries. At first sight there is no reason to believe that the colonies named are not the ones to which the servant was destined, but when indenture forms are compared with their entries in the register some discrepancies can be seen. Until 1724 this does not appear to have been a serious problem and over 96 per cent of destinations in the register that can be checked for this period correspond to those on the indenture forms, and the inaccuracies can probably be attributed to copying errors. However, after 1724 it appears to have been the practice of the clerks who made the register to take a bundle of indenture forms drawn up by an agent during a particular month and to enter the destination from just one of them as the destination for the whole group, even when a variety of destinations were involved. Nevertheless, a comparison of indenture forms and register entries for the period after 1724 shows that where they can be checked, 79.4 per cent are accurate. This is to be expected, given the fact that an agent would at any one time be likely to be gathering a group of servants to send on a particular ship. In addition, a comparison has been made of the overall pattern of indenture form destinations and the destinations of the servants who appear only in the register, and the results can be seen in the following table. Although there are differences in the pattern of destinations they are not very great, and the main problems appear to affect Antigua and St. Lucia/St. Christopher.

	INDENTURES		REGISTER	
	no	%	no	%
Antigua	55	2.7	118	7.6
Barbados	28	1.4	15	1.0
Jamaica	647	32.2	567	36.7
St. Lucia/St. Christopher	125	6.2	2	0.1
Other West Indies	13	0.6	11	0.7
Carolinas	18	0.9	15	1.0
Maryland	632	31.4	455	29.5
Pennsylvania	198	9.9	218	14.1
Virginia	165	8.2	115	7.5
Other North America	120	6.0	18	1.2
N.D. or unclear	9	0.4	10	0.6
Total	2010		1544	

A comparison of destinations given on indenture forms with destinations given in the register for entries which have no surviving indenture form, 1718-33.

Any interpretation of the destination data must take the preceding analysis into account, although the destinations are likely to be accurate in four out of five cases. However, in those cases where an agent is listed with only one servant, it may be assumed that the destination is accurate, and these destinations are given in capitals.

Page Numbers

The final column in the lists gives the folio number in the register where the entry is located and *v* indicates that it is to be found on the reverse side of that page.

APPENDIX TO PART TWO

Act of Parliament: 4 George I C.11 A.D. 1717

An Act for the further preventing Robbery, Burglary and other Felonies, and for the more effectual Transportation of Felons, and unlawful Exporters of Wool; and for declaring the Law upon some points relating to Pirates.

Clause V

"And whereas there are many idle Persons, who are under the Age of One and twenty Years, lurking about in divers Parts of LONDON, and elsewhere, who want Employment, and may be tempted to become Thieves, if not provided for: And whereas they may be inclined to be transported, and to enter into Services in some of His Majesty's Colonies and Plantations in AMERICA; but as they have no Power to contract for themselves and therefore that it is not safe for Merchants to transport them, or take them into such Services;" Be it enacted by the Authority aforesaid, That where any Person of the Age of Fifteen Years or more, and under the Age of Twenty one, shall be willing to be transported, and to enter into any Service in any of His Majesty's Colonies or Plantations in AMERICA, it shall and may be lawful for any Merchant, or other, to contract with any such Person for any such Service, not exceeding the Term of Eight Years; provided such person so binding him or herself do come before the Lord Mayor of LONDON, or some other Justice of the Peace of the

City, if such Contract be made within the same, or the Liberties thereof, or before some other Two Justices of the Peace of the Place where such Contract shall be made, if made elsewhere, and before such Magistrate or Magistrates acknowledge such Content, and do sign such Contract in his or their Presence, and with his or their Approbation; and that then it shall be lawful for any such Merchant or other, to transport such Person so binding him or herself, and to keep him or her within any of the said Plantations or Colonies, according to the Tenor of such Contract as aforesaid; any Law or Statute to the contrary in any wise notwithstanding; which said Contract and Approbation of such Magistrate or Magistrates, with the tenor of such Contract, shall be certified by such Magistrate or Magistrates to the next General Quarter-Sessions of the Peace, held for that County where such Magistrate or Magistrates shall reside, to be registered by the Clerk of the Peace without Fee or Reward.

Clause IX

And be it also enacted, That this Act shall extend to all His Majesty's Dominions in AMERICA, and shall be taken as a Publick Act.

PART THREE

A LIST OF EMIGRANTS
FROM LONDON TO AMERICA
1718-1733

A

1	ABBETT, John	Peter Simpson	Pennsylvania	16 Oct 1727	31
2	ABBITTS, Thomas	Capt Nathaniel Stisson	ANTIGUA	13 Oct 1729	41v
3	ABLEY, Richard	James Gerald	Pennsylvania	15 Jul 1728	35
4	ADAM, Robert	John Taylor	Maryland	10 Oct 1726	27v
5	ADAMS, Ann	John Cooke	Pennsylvania	25 Aug 1725	20v
6	ADAMS, Hannah	John Cooke	Pennsylvania	25 Aug 1725	20v
7	ADAMS, Thomas	John Ball	Maryland	14 Oct 1728	37
8	ADIN, William	Samuel Gloynes	Maryland	22 Feb 1726	19v
9	ADKINSON, William	Peter Simpson	Maryland	Dec 1732	61v
10	ADSHEAD, Thomas	Neal MacNeal	Jamaica	Sep 1732	60v
11	AISHFORD, Thomas	Samuel Gloynes	Maryland	13 Jan 1726	17v
12	AKERMAN, William	James Gerald	Maryland	4 Dec 1727	32
13	ALDERTON, John	Neal MacNeal	Maryland	Dec 1732	61v
14	ALDRIDGE, Daniel	John Ball	Pennsylvania	16 Oct 1727	30v
15	ALFORD, George	John Taylor	Jamaica	5 Apr 1725	20
16	ALLEN, George	Neal MacNeal	Jamaica	Jul 1732	60
17	ALLEN, James	Samuel Gloynes	Maryland	13 Jan 1726	17v
18	ALLEN, Thomas	Thomas Nixson	Maryland	Jan 1732	57v
19	ALLESTREE, John	John Taylor	Jamaica	5 Apr 1725	19v
20	ALLEY, Nathaniel	James Gerald	Maryland	13 Jan 1726	18v
21	AMOR, John	John Taylor	Jamaica	5 Dec 1726	19
22	ANDERSON, Elizabeth	Peter Simpson	Virginia	14 Oct 1728	37
23	ANDREW, Thomas	John Taylor	Maryland	10 Oct 1726	27v
24	ANDREWS, James	Neal MacNeal	Maryland	Mar 1733	59v
25	ANDRIEN, James	John Dykes	Maryland	13 Jan 1726	17v
26	ANNAN, John	Peter Simpson	Maryland	26 Feb 1729	32v
27	ANNS, Charles	James Gerald	Jamaica	Feb 1727	49v
28	ANTHONY, Robert	John Cooke	Virginia	13 Jan 1726	18
29	ARCHER, William	John Cooke	Jamaica	5 Dec 1726	29
30	ARMESTRONG, John	James Gerald	Maryland	13 Jan 1726	18v

31	ARMITAGE, James	Peter Simpson	Jamaica	Dec 1731	55
32	ARMSTRONG, James	James Gerald	Pennsylvania	15 Jul 1728	35
33	ARMSTRONG, Joseph	Peter Simpson	Virginia	16 Oct 1727	30
34	ARMSTRONG, Moses	Neal MacNeal	Pennsylvania	Feb 1733	59
35	ARNOTT, Francis	John Taylor	Jamaica	Feb 1732	58
36	ARNOTT, Mary	Capt Edward Hickes	JAMAICA	Sep 1732	60v
37	ASHBY, William	James Gerald	Pennsylvania	Jan 1733	58v
38	ATKINS, Charles	James Gerald	Maryland	18 Apr 1726	26
39	ATKINS, John	James Gerald	Maryland	18 Apr 1726	25v
40	ATKINS, Thomas	James Gerald	Antigua	2 Dec 1728	38v
41	ATKINSON, Edward	William Burge	Jamaica	Feb 1731	54
42	ATKINSON, William	Neal MacNeal	Maryland	Mar 1733	59v
43	ATTKINSON, Richard	William Burge	Virginia	Dec 1732	62
44	ATTLEBURN, Thomas	Samuel Gloynes	Jamaica	6 Dec 1725	24
45	ATWICKS, Thomas	William Burge	Antigua	2 Dec 1728	38v
46	AUDLEY, Edward	James Gerald	Jamaica	6 Dec 1725	23v
47	AUSTYN, George	James Gerald	Pennsylvania	15 Jul 1728	35
48	AVIS, James	John Taylor	Jamaica	20 Jul 1726	26v
49	AYRES, John	Neal MacNeal	Maryland	Feb 1727	49v

B

50	BADGE, Thomas	Peter Simpson	Maryland	5 Dec 1726	28v
51	BADLEY, Robert	John Taylor	Jamaica	11 Oct 1725	21
52	BAILEY, John	James Gerald	Jamaica	10 Oct 1726	27v
53	BAILEY, Henry	John Taylor	Maryland	6 Dec 1725	24v
54	BAILY, James	John Taylor	Jamaica	14 Apr 1729	40
55	BAINES, John	John Taylor	Jamaica	28 Feb 1727	25v
56	BAKER, Elizabeth	Peter Simpson	Jamaica	Dec 1731	55
57	BAKER, Phillip	John Taylor	South Carolina	May 1732	60
58	BAKER, Sarah	John Ball	Pennsylvania	16 Oct 1727	30v
59	BALL, John	John Taylor	Jamaica	2 Dec 1728	38
60	BALL, William	Thomas Mixon	VIRGINIA	14 Apr 1729	40
61	BALLESTONE, Thomas	John Cooke	Pennsylvania	18 Apr 1726	26
62	BALLITT, Charles	James Gerald	Pennsylvania	Jan 1732	57v
63	BAMBRIDGE, Robert	John Taylor	Jamaica	14 Oct 1728	37v
64	BAMFORD, Thomas	Peter Simpson	Jamaica	Dec 1731	55
65	BANFORD, Marmaduke	Christopher Veale	ST CHRISTOPHER OR ST LUCIA	3 Sep 1722	11
66	BANKS, Michael	William Burge	PENNSYLVANIA	11 Jan 1728	29v
67	BARLOW, Thomas	John Ball	Jamaica	14 Oct 1728	36v
68	BARNARD, Henry	John Ball	Maryland	29 Apr 1728	33v
69	BARNBY, John	Peter Simpson	Antigua	14 Oct 1728	36v
70	BARNET, Thomas	James Gerald	Jamaica	6 Dec 1725	24
71	BARNETT, John	John Taylor	Jamaica	10 Oct 1726	27
72	BARTLET, Francis	John Cooke	Pennsylvania	18 Apr 1726	25v
73	BARTON, John	Samuel Gloynes	Jamaica	6 Dec 1725	24v
74	BASSETT, George	John Taylor	Jamaica	25 Aug 1729	41
75	BATCHELOR, John	Peter Simpson	Maryland	5 Dec 1726	28v
76	BATEMAN, Samuel	Richard Bateman	Jamaica	13 Jan 1726	17v
77	BATES, Edward	William Cash	Virginia	6 Dec 1725	25
78	BATES, Henry	Christopher Veale	MARYLAND	15 Jan 1724	14

79	BATES, Isaac	Peter Simpson	Maryland	2 Dec 1728	38v
80	BATTAWAY, Thomas	Peter Simpson	Pennsylvania	16 Oct 1727	31
81	BAXTER, William	Peter Simpson	Pennsylvania	13 Oct 1729	41v
82	BAYLEY, Richard	Samuel Gloynes	Jamaica	6 Dec 1725	24
83	BEALE, John	Samuel Gloynes	Jamaica	6 Dec 1725	24
84	BEALES, Edward	Peter Simpson	Maryland	10 Oct 1726	27v
85	BEAMOUNT, Timothy	Peter Simpson	Jamaica	Jan 1733	58v
86	BEAVANS, Benjamin	James Gerald	Maryland	18 Apr 1726	26
87	BECHAM, Elizabeth	Peter Simpson	Maryland	5 Dec 1726	28v
88	BECK, James	Peter Simpson	Maryland	12 Jan 1727	25
89	BECKET, George	John Ball	Pennsylvania	16 Oct 1727	30
90	BECKET, William	John Ball	Antigua	2 Dec 1728	39
91	BECKETT, Johanason	John Cooke	Virginia	13 Jan 1726	18
92	BECKFORD, Mary	Capt Christopher Cowton	MARYLAND	15 Jan 1724	13v
93	BEDFORD, John	John Taylor	Jamaica	28 Feb 1727	25v
94	BEEBY, William	John Cooke	Jamaica	10 Oct 1726	27
95	BEECHAMP, John	John Taylor	Jamaica	16 Feb 1729	33v
96	BEEDLE, John	Joseph Whilton	Pennsylvania	26 Feb 1729	33
97	BEERBRIDGE, Timothy	John Dykes	PENNSYLVANIA	11 Oct 1725	21v
98	BELSON, Abraham	James Gerald	Maryland	13 Jan 1726	18v
99	BENBRIDGE, Robert	Samuel Gloynes	Maryland	13 Jan 1726	18
100	BENNETT, George	William Cash	Virginia	6 Dec 1725	25
101	BENNETT, George	James Gerald	MARYLAND	Mar 1727	49v
102	BENNETT, John	John Taylor	MARYLAND	15 Jan 1724	13v
103	BENNY, Richard	William Burge	Jamaica	Jan 1731	52
104	BERCLAY, James	John Taylor	Jamaica	10 Oct 1726	27
105	BEREY, Edward	Christopher Veale	VIRGINIA	5 Apr 1725	19v
106	BERMETT, George	John Cooke	Jamaica	9 Aug 1726	27
107	BERRY, William	John Cooke	Maryland	22 Feb 1726	19
108	BETTS, John	Peter Simpson	Maryland	Dec 1732	61v
109	BETTS, Robert	Samuel Gloynes	Jamaica	6 Dec 1725	24

110	BETTY, Robert	John Taylor	Jamaica	Jul 1732	60
111	BEVEERE, Abraham	John Dykes	Pennsylvania	25 Aug 1725	21
112	BIGNALL, Joseph	John Ball	Maryland	4 Dec 1727	31v
113	BINGHAM, Samuel	James Gerald	Maryland	13 Jan 1726	19
114	BIRD, John	John Taylor	Jamaica	5 Apr 1725	20
115	BIRD, John	Peter Simpson	Maryland	Dec 1732	61v
116	BIRD, Samuel	John Taylor	N.D.	13 Oct 1718	2
117	BIRD, William	James Gerald	JAMAICA	14 Apr 1729	40
118	BIRKHEAD, John	Richard White	Maryland	14 Feb 1730	39v
119	BIRON, Thomas	Peter Simpson	Barbados	Feb 1733	59
120	BISHOP, James	John Taylor	Jamaica	10 Oct 1726	27
121	BISHOP, Thomas	James Gerald	Maryland	13 Jan 1726	18v
122	BLACK, William	James Gerald	Maryland	13 Jan 1726	18v
123	BLACKHALL, Thomas	Peter Simpson	Maryland	Dec 1731	54v
124	BLAIR, David	James Gerald	NEVIS	15 Jan 1724	14
125	BLAKE, John	Humphrey Bell	VIRGINIA	14 Apr 1729	40
126	BLAKESLY, Robert	Peter Simpson	MARYLAND	11 Jan 1728	29v
127	BLANCHARD, John	Samuel Gloynes	Jamaica	6 Dec 1725	24
128	BLODEN, John	John Taylor	Pennsylvania	28 Aug 1727	29v
129	BLUCK, John	John Taylor	Jamaica	10 Oct 1726	27
130	BLYTH, William	James Gerald	Maryland	14 Oct 1728	37v
131	BONE, William	Peter Simpson	New England	Nov 1732	61v
132	BOONE, John	John Taylor	Pennsylvania	Dec 1730	45
133	BOOTH, Benjamin	James Gerald	Jamaica	6 Dec 1725	23v
134	BORDMAN, Elizabeth	Samuel Gloynes	Virginia	4 Dec 1727	32
135	BOUCHAU, Philip	Peter Simpson	Maryland	18 Apr 1726	26
136	BOUDRY, John	Peter Simpson	Jamaica	Aug 1732	60v
137	BOUGHTON, John	Peter Simpson	Jamaica	Jun 1732	60
138	BOULTON, Francis	Peter Simpson	Maryland	Dec 1732	61v
139	BOURGEIN, Barnaby	James Gerald	Jamaica	6 Dec 1725	23v
140	BOURNE, Henry	John Taylor	Jamaica	7 Jul 1729	40v

141	BOHANNAN, Isaac	William Cash	ANTIGUA	14 Oct 1728	37
142	BOWER, Jonathan	William Williams	SOUTH CAROLINA	28 Aug 1727	30
143	BOWERS, Samuel	John Taylor	Jamaica	28 Feb 1727	25v
144	BOWES, John	John Taylor	Jamaica	2 Dec 1728	38
145	BOWLER, James	Peter Simpson	Maryland	Dec 1731	54v
146	BOWMAN, John	William Cash	Antigua	2 Dec 1728	38v
147	BRADFIELD, John	Neal MacNeal	Jamaica	Aug 1732	60v
148	BRADFORD, Hannah	Samuel Gloynes	Virginia	4 Dec 1727	32
149	BRADFORD, Richard	Neal MacNeal	Pennsylvania	Feb 1733	59
150	BRADIS, Richard	John Cooke	Jamaica	6 Dec 1725	24v
151	BRADLEY, Henry	Peter Simpson	Maryland	Dec 1731	54v
152	BRANDON, Charles	Neal MacNeal	Maryland	Jan 1732	57v
153	BRANDON, William	John Taylor	Maryland	6 Dec 1725	24v
154	BRANFORD, Ambrose	John Ball	Antigua	2 Dec 1728	38
155	BRATON, John	Neal MacNeal	Jamaica	Jun 1732	60
156	BRAWDON, Michael	James Gerald	Maryland	13 Jan 1726	18v
157	BRAY, William	John Taylor	Jamaica	2 Dec 1728	38
158	BRAZIER, Richard	John Ball	Jamaica	15 Jan 1729	32v
159	BREESE, John	John Taylor	Pennsylvania	16 Oct 1727	30v
160	BRICE, William	John Ball	Antigua	2 Dec 1728	38
161	BRIDGE, John	John Taylor	Jamaica	10 Oct 1726	27
162	BRIDGE, Patrick	James Gerald	Maryland	13 Jan 1726	19
163	BRIDGES, Joseph	Peter Simpson	Pennsylvania	16 Oct 1727	31
164	BRIGGS, Henry	Bartholomew Voakes	N.D.	25 Aug 1725	20v
165	BRIGGS, John	John Taylor	Pennsylvania	28 Aug 1727	29v
166	BRIGGS, John	John Ball	Antigua	2 Dec 1728	38
167	BRIGHTREE, Thomas	Richard White	Nevis	Nov 1729	48
168	BRISCOE, Henry	John Taylor	Jamaica	23 May 1726	26v
169	BRISCOE, John	John Taylor	Jamaica	5 Apr 1725	20
170	BRITTAIN, Thomas	John Cooke	Maryland	22 Feb 1726	19v
171	BROAD, Thomas	John Dykes	Pennsylvania	25 Aug 1725	21

172	BROADMEAD, William	John Taylor	Pennsylvania	16 Oct 1727	30v
173	BRODIE, Richard	Richard Bateman	Jamaica	13 Jan 1726	17v
174	BROMLEY, Richard	Neal MacNeal	Jamaica	Nov 1732	61
175	BROOKING, Charles	John Taylor	Jamaica	Jul 1732	60
176	BROOKS, Daniel	John Taylor	Jamaica	Jan 1733	58v
177	BROOKS, Daniel	James Gerald	Jamaica	11 Oct 1725	21v
178	BROOKS, Ralph	James Gerald	Pennsylvania	Jan 1733	58v
179	BROOKS, Thomas	John Cooke	Jamaica	9 Aug 1726	27
180	BROOM, Joseph	John Ball	Pennsylvania	16 Oct 1727	30
181	BROUGHTON, Nathaniel	James Gerald	Pennsylvania	25 Aug 1729	41
182	BROUGHTON, Richard	John Cooke	Jamaica	10 Oct 1726	27v
183	BROWN, Ann	John Ball	Pennsylvania	16 Oct 1727	30v
184	BROWN, Edward	John Cooke	Maryland	5 Dec 1726	28v
185	BROWN, Henry	Neal MacNeal	Antigua	25 Aug 1729	41
186	BROWN, James	Peter Simpson	MARYLAND	29 Apr 1728	33v
187	BROWN, James	John Ball	Jamaica	14 Oct 1728	36v
188	BROWN, John	James Gerald	Jamaica	6 Dec 1725	24
189	BROWN, John	John Taylor	Maryland	13 Jan 1726	17v
190	BROWN, John	James Gerald	Maryland	18 Apr 1726	25v
191	BROWN, John	John Ball	Pennsylvania	16 Oct 1727	30v
192	BROWN, John	Peter Simpson	Maryland	2 Dec 1728	38v
193	BROWN, John	Joseph Whilton	Pennsylvania	26 Feb 1729	33
194	BROWN, John	John Taylor	CAROLINA	Aug 1732	60v
195	BROWN, John	Peter Simpson	Jamaica	Aug 1732	60v
196	BROWN, Mary	John Cooke	Jamaica	5 Dec 1726	29
197	BROWN, Matthew	Christopher Veale	Virginia	5 Apr 1725	20
198	BROWN, Michael	John Ball	Pennsylvania	16 Oct 1727	30v
199	BROWN, Nathaniel	John Taylor	Pennsylvania	16 Oct 1727	30v
200	BROWN, Richard	William Burge	Pennsylvania	29 Apr 1728	33v
201	BROWN, Thomas	Samuel Gloynes	Maryland	13 Jan 1726	18
202	BROWN, Thomas	Richard White	Antigua	13 Oct 1729	42

203	BROWNE, John	Peter Simpson	Jamaica		Jan 1731	52ν
204	BROWNE, Stephen	John Ball	Antigua	2 Dec 1728	39
205	BRYAN, Edward	John Taylor	Jamaica	2 Dec 1728	38
206	BRYENTON, Gregory	James Gerald	Antigua		Jan 1727	49ν
207	BUCHANAN, William	Neal MacNeal	Jamaica		May 1732	59ν
208	BUCKINGHAM, Richard	John Taylor	Jamaica		Mar 1733	59ν
209	BUCKLEY, James	John Taylor	Jamaica	13 Oct 1729	42
210	BUCKLEY, John	Joseph Whilton	Antigua	13 Oct 1729	42
211	BULLEN, Edward	Neal MacNeal	Jamaica		May 1732	59ν
212	BULLMAN, William	John Taylor	Jamaica		Dec 1732	62
213	BURCH, Denis	John Cooke	Maryland	5 Dec 1726	28ν
214	BURDEN, Francis	Neal MacNeal	Antigua	13 Oct 1729	41ν
215	BURDEN, Thomas	Peter Simpson	Barbados		Feb 1733	59
216	BURGES, James	Neal MacNeal	Jamaica	7 Jul 1729	40ν
217	BURGESS, William	John Cooke	Jamaica	10 Oct 1726	27
218	BURGOYNE, Jane	Peter Simpson	Jamaica		Dec 1731	55
219	BURHAM, Cavantage	William Burge	Maryland		Mar 1733	59
220	BURNHAM, Henry	John Taylor	Pennsylvania	28 Aug 1727	29ν
221	BURRAGE, Edward	Neal MacNeal	Maryland		Jan 1732	57ν
222	BURT, John	Neal MacNeal	Pennsylvania		Feb 1733	59
223	BURT, Stephen	John Ball	Jamaica	14 Oct 1728	36ν
224	BURTON, Richard	John Cooke	Virginia	13 Jan 1726	18ν
225	BURTON, Thomas	William Burge	Antigua	2 Dec 1728	38ν
226	BUSH, Thomas	John Taylor	Pennsylvania	16 Oct 1727	30ν
227	BUTCHER, John	John Taylor	Maryland	6 Dec 1725	25
228	BUTLER, Alice Agness	Peter Simpson	Maryland	5 Dec 1726	28ν
229	BUTLER, Richard	John Taylor	Jamaica	25 Aug 1729	41
230	BUTT, Benjamin	Neal MacNeal	Jamaica		Sep 1732	60ν
231	BUTT, John	Peter Simpson	Maryland	2 Dec 1728	38ν
232	BUTTERE, Henry	John Ball	Antigua	2 Dec 1728	38
233	BUTTERETH, John	Neal MacNeal	Jamaica		Mar 1732	58

234	BUTTERFIELD, William	John Dykes	MARYLAND	15 Jan 1724	14
235	BUTTERY, Christopher	Christopher Veale	NORTH CAROLINA	15 Jan 1724	14
236	BUTWELL, Thomas	Peter Simpson	Pennsylvania	13 Oct 1729	41v
237	BYERS, Edward	John Taylor	Jamaica	10 Oct 1726	27
238	BYRCH, Joseph	William Cash	Maryland	1 Dec 1729	42v

C

239	CAIN, John	John Taylor	South Carolina	May 1732	60
240	CAINE, Henry	Richard Bateman	Jamaica	13 Jan 1726	17v
241	CAIRSTIERS, John	John Ball	Maryland	14 Oct 1728	37
242	CALF, John	Peter Simpson	Maryland	15 Jan 1729	32v
243	CALLABRE, Stephen	John Taylor	Jamaica	20 Jul 1726	26v
244	CALLAWAY, James	William Cash	Pennsylvania	29 Apr 1728	33v
245	CALLOW, Edward	Peter Simpson	Maryland	5 Dec 1726	28v
246	CAMBELL, William	Peter Simpson	Maryland	4 Dec 1727	31v
247	CAMEL, Alexander	John Ball	Pennsylvania	16 Oct 1727	30v
248	CAMERON, James	James Gerald	Antigua	Jan 1727	49v
249	CAMLES, Nathaniel	Peter Simpson	MARYLAND	10 Apr 1727	29v
250	CAMMELL, Robert	William Burge	Antigua	13 Oct 1729	41v
251	CAMPBELL, Alexander	James Gerald	Pennsylvania	15 Jul 1728	35
252	CAMPBELL, Archebald	Wiliam Cash	Maryland	14 Oct 1728	37v
253	CAMPBELL, John	John Taylor	Jamaica	Oct 1732	61
254	CAMPBELL, John	Neal MacNeal	Jamaica	Nov 1732	61
255	CANABY, John	William Burge	Virginia	14 Apr 1729	40
256	CANNON, William	Peter Simpson	Maryland	14 Jan 1730	39v
257	CAPLIN, James	John Taylor	Jamaica	10 Oct 1726	27
258	CARLETON, Thomas	Neal MacNeal	Antigua	13 Oct 1729	41v
259	CARPENTER, Humphry	John Taylor	Jamaica	12 Jan 1727	25
260	CARSLY, John	John Taylor	Jamaica	5 Apr 1725	20
261	CARTER, Christopher	John Dykes	Pennsylvania	25 Aug 1725	21
262	CARTER, Edmund	John Taylor	Jamaica	14 Apr 1729	40
263	CARTER, Jeremia	John Dykes	MARYLAND	15 Jan 1724	14
264	CARTER, John	John Taylor	Antigua	13 Oct 1729	42
265	CARY, William	John Cooke	Pennsylvania	18 Apr 1726	25v
266	CASALTON, Edward	James Gerald	Jamaica	6 Dec 1725	24
267	CASEBURN, John	Isaac Stiff	Jamaica	Jan 1731	53
268	CATE, John	Peter Simpson	Barbados	Feb 1733	59

269	CHADELTON, Richard	Neal MacNeal	Jamaica	Jul 1732	60
270	CHALLIS, Thomas	John Taylor	Jamaica	18 Apr 1726	26
271	CHAMBERLEN, Paul	Peter Simpson	Maryland	14 Jan 1730	39v
272	CHAMBERS, George	Richard White	Maryland	14 Feb 1730	39v
273	CHAMBERS, James	Richard White	Maryland	14 Feb 1730	39v
274	CHAMBERS, John	Peter Simpson	Maryland	Dec 1731	54v
275	CHAMBERS, Richard	Neal MacNeal	Jamaica	May 1731	55v
276	CHANTANVICUX, Paul	Jonathan Forward	Virginia	Dec 1732	62
277	CHAPMAN, Cornelius	Peter Simpson	MARYLAND	Oct 1732	61
278	CHAPMAN, Richard	Samuel Gloynes	Maryland	13 Jan 1726	18
279	CHAPMAN, Richard	Peter Simpson	MARYLAND	4 Dec 1727	31v
280	CHARLETT, John	Peter Simpson	Virginia	14 Oct 1728	37
281	CHESHIRE, John	Samuel Gloynes	Jamaica	6 Dec 1725	24
282	CHESTERS, Robert	John Ball	Antigua	2 Dec 1728	38
283	CHEVERTON, Thomas	John Cooke	Virginia	10 Oct 1726	28
284	CHEYNE, James	John Cooke	Maryland	22 Feb 1726	19
285	CHIMMO, John	John Cooke	Virginia	13 Jan 1726	18
286	CHRISTIAN, Elizabeth	John Cooke	Pennsylvania	5 Apr 1725	20
287	CLARIDGE, Witherstone	John Taylor	Jamaica	Jan 1733	58v
288	CLARK, James	John Taylor	Jamaica	7 Jul 1729	40v
289	CLARK, Peter	Peter Simpson	Jamaica	Dec 1731	55
290	CLARK, Richard	William Burge	Antigua	14 Oct 1728	37v
291	CLARK, Thomas	John Taylor	Jamaica	5 Apr 1725	20
292	CLARK, Thomas	James Gerald	Jamaica	14 Oct 1728	37
293	CLARK, William	John Cooke	Virginia	10 Oct 1726	28
294	CLARKE, John	Neal MacNeal	Jamaica	Nov 1732	61
295	CLARKE, William	Peter Simpson	Antigua	14 Oct 1728	36v
296	CLARKE, William	Neal MacNeal	Maryland	Jan 1732	57v
297	CLARKE, William	Neal MacNeal	Jamaica	Aug 1732	60v
298	CLARKSON, Charles	James Gerald	Jamaica	12 Jan 1727	25
299	CLAY, Alexander	John Ball	Antigua	2 Dec 1728	38

300	CLAYPOLE, Henry	James Gerald	Pennsylvania	15 Jul 1728	35
301	CLEARK, Robert	John Ball	Maryland	29 Apr 1728	33v
302	CLEAVER, Robert	James Gerald	Jamaica	16 Oct 1727	31
303	CLEMENT, Thomas	John Taylor	Jamaica	5 Apr 1725	20
304	CLEMENTS, Joseph	William Cash	Maryland	14 Oct 1728	37v
305	CLIFTON, George	Samuel Gloynes	Maryland	11 Jan 1728	29
306	CLIFTON, Moses	John Taylor	Jamaica	Jan 1731	53
307	CLOSE, William	John Taylor	Jamaica	26 Feb 1729	33
308	COARVELL, George	James Gerald	Antigua	Jan 1727	49v
309	COATES, Nathaniel	John Taylor	Jamaica	18 Apr 1726	26
310	COCK, Charles	William Burge	Jamaica	Sep 1731	51
311	COCKETT, Daniel	William Trottman	New England	Dec 1732	62
312	COCKRAM, James	John Magier	MARYLAND	Dec 1731	55
313	COCKS, John	William Cash	Antigua	26 Aug 1728	35v
314	COCTERAM, James	Slingsby Bethell	ANTIGUA	5 Dec 1726	29
315	COLE, Michael	John Ball	Maryland	14 Oct 1728	37
316	COLE, Thomas	John Taylor	Jamaica	5 Apr 1725	19v
317	COLE, William	Samuel Gloynes	Maryland	2 Dec 1728	38v
318	COLES, Edward	Samuel Gloynes	Pennsylvania	18 Apr 1726	26
319	COLLET, James	John Taylor	Jamaica	Feb 1733	59
320	COLLEY, Thomas	John Taylor	Jamaica	14 Oct 1728	37v
321	COLLINS, Henry	James Gerald	Maryland	13 Jan 1726	18v
322	COLLINS, Jonas	Peter Simpson	Antigua	14 Oct 1728	36v
323	COLLYER, James	Peter Simpson	Antigua	2 Dec 1728	38v
324	COLVIN, George	Peter Simpson	Jamaica	Dec 1731	55
325	COMBS, James	John Taylor	Jamaica	9 Aug 1726	27
326	CONNELLY, Thomas	Peter Simpson	Maryland	2 Dec 1728	38v
327	COOK, Alexander	William Burge	Jamaica	Feb 1731	54
328	COOK, Ann	John Ball	Maryland	4 Dec 1727	31v
329	COOK, Edward	John Taylor	Jamaica	Jul 1732	60
330	COOK, Edward	Neal MacNeal	Jamaica	Jan 1733	58

331	COOK, Francis	John Taylor	Jamaica	22 Feb 1726	19v
332	COOK, Stephen	John Taylor	Maryland	6 Dec 1724	24v
333	COOKE, John	Samuel Gloynes	Jamaica	6 Dec 1725	24
334	COOPER, Edmund	Samuel Gloynes	Virginia	4 Dec 1727	32
335	COOPER, Francis	James Gerald	Maryland	10 Oct 1726	28
336	COOPER, Henry	John Taylor	Jamaica	26 Feb 1729	33
337	COOPER, Joseph	John Cooke	Jamaica	5 Dec 1726	29
338	COPPINGER, Nicholas	John Taylor	Jamaica	25 Aug 1729	41
339	CORBETT, Charles	Samuel Gloynes	Virginia	4 Dec 1727	32
340	CORBETT, Oswald	William Cash	Pennsylvania	29 Apr 1728	33v
341	CORDEL, Peter	Samuel Gloynes	Pennsylvania	18 Apr 1726	26
342	CORDEROY, John	John Taylor	Maryland	6 Dec 1725	24v
343	CORP, Charles	John Taylor	Jamaica	Oct 1732	61
344	CORRIE, Alexander	Neal MacNeal	Maryland	Dec 1732	62
345	CORSAN, William	Neal MacNeal	Jamaica	Jan 1733	58
346	COSBEY, John	John Cooke	Jamaica	5 Dec 1726	29
347	COSINS, Thomas	James Gerald	Maryland	Nov 1732	61
348	COT, Horsman	James Gerald	Pennsylvania	15 Jul 1728	35
349	COURCELLE, Peter	Neal MacNeal	Maryland	Mar 1733	59v
350	COUSZINS, Thomas	John Ball	Jamaica	26 Feb 1729	33
351	COUTS, Thomas	John Cooke	Virginia	13 Jan 1726	18v
352	COWARD, John	Peter Simpson	Jamaica	Jan 1733	58v
353	COWCRAFT, George	William Burge	Antigua	26 Aug 1728	36
354	COWLEY, Edward	John Cooke	Jamaica	10 Oct 1726	27
355	COX, Jonathan	Peter Simpson	Maryland	5 Dec 1726	28v
356	COX, Joseph	Richard Bateman	Maryland	6 Dec 1725	25
357	COX, Mary	John Cooke	Pennsylvania	25 Aug 1725	20v
358	COZGROVE, Christopher	James Gerald	Pennsylvania	15 Jul 1728	35
359	CRADDOCK, Henry	John Cooke	Jamaica	6 Dec 1725	24v
360	CRADDOCK, James	John Taylor	South Carolina	Mar 1732	58
361	CRADDOCK, Mary	James Gerald	Jamaica	11 Oct 1725	21v

362	CRAFTS, William	Neal MacNeal	Maryland	Jan 1732	57v
363	CRAIGHTON, John	Peter Simpson	Jamaica	10 Oct 1726	27v
364	CRAVEN, Thomas	Neal MacNeal	Maryland	Jan 1732	57v
365	CRAWFORD, Charles	Samuel Gloynes	Maryland	2 Dec 1728	38v
366	CREESE, William	Richard White	Antigua	13 Oct 1729	42v
367	CRESY, George	John Cooke	Jamaica	6 Dec 1725	24v
368	CRISP, William	John Ball	Maryland	14 Oct 1728	37
369	CROCKFORD, Micah	James Gerald	Maryland	14 Oct 1728	37v
370	CROKER, Daniel	John Cooke	Jamaica	9 Aug 1726	27
371	CROPP, Samuel	William Cash	Maryland	26 Feb 1729	32v
372	CROSS , James	Neal MacNeal	Jamaica	Nov 1732	61
373	CROSS, Richard	John Taylor	Jamaica	Mar 1731	54
374	CROSS, Samuel	John Cooke	Pennsylvania	25 Aug 1725	20v
375	CROSS, Stephen	John Dykes	NEW ENGLAND	May 1720	5v
376	CROW, Henry	John Cooke	Maryland	22 Feb 1726	19
377	CROWCH, Richard	John Cooke	Virginia	13 Jan 1726	18
378	CULBERSTON, Andrew	James Gerald	Jamaica	6 Dec 1725	24
379	CUNISBY, John	Peter Simpson	Jamaica	Jul 1732	60
380	CUSSENS, Leonard	James Gerald	Pennsylvania	25 Aug 1725	21
381	CUTHBERT, John	Peter Simpson	Jamaica	Dec 1731	55
382	CUTS, Thomas	James Gerald	Maryland	13 Jan 1726	18v
383	CUTTS, Alexander	Capt Nathaniel Stisson	ANTIGUA	13 Oct 1729	41v

D

384	DAGGET, Rachel	Peter Simpson	JAMAICA	Mar 1727	49v
385	DAHAY, David	Peter Simpson	Maryland	10 Oct 1726	27v
386	DAREY, Joseph	John Cooke	Maryland	5 Dec 1726	28v
387	DARLEY, Andrew	James Gerald	Pennsylvania	15 Jul 1728	35
388	DARWOOD, George	Neal MacNeal	Antigua	13 Oct 1729	42
389	DAVIES, John	Peter Simpson	Pennsylvania	13 Oct 1729	41v
390	DAVIS, Ann	Peter Simpson	Maryland	18 Apr 1726	26
391	DAVIS, Arthur	Peter Simpson	New England	Nov 1732	61v
392	DAVIS, John	Peter Simpson	Maryland	5 Dec 1726	28v
393	DAVIS, Joseph	John Taylor	Jamaica	26 Feb 1729	33
394	DAVIS, Matthew	James Gerald	Virginia	5 Dec 1726	29
395	DAVIS, Owen	Peter Simpson	Maryland	14 Jan 1730	39v
396	DAVIS, Robert	John Cooke	Jamaica	10 Oct 1726	27v
397	DAVIS, Samuel	John Taylor	Jamaica	Jan 1731	53
398	DAVIS, William	Samuel Gloynes	Maryland	13 Jan 1726	18
399	DAVIS, William	John Ball	Maryland	4 Dec 1727	31v
400	DAWKINS, Jeremiah	John Taylor	Jamaica	Oct 1732	61
401	DAWSBERRY, John	John Ball	Pennsylvania	16 Oct 1727	30v
402	DAY, George	John Taylor	Jamaica	Jan 1731	53
403	DEAN, William	Peter Simpson	Pennsylvania	13 Oct 1729	41v
404	DEANE, Francis	John Taylor	Jamaica	2 Dec 1728	38
405	DEARLOVE, Thomas	John Taylor	Jamaica	Oct 1732	61
406	DEDRICK, John Christian	Richard Bateman	Maryland	6 Dec 1725	25
407	DEFERME, Jasper	Samuel Gloynes	Maryland	13 Jan 1726	18
408	DELAPORTE, Peter	John Cooke	Jamaica	5 Dec 1726	29
409	DE MALDEGREA, Francis	Richard Bateman	Maryland	22 Feb 1726	19
410	DENNIS, William	James Gerald	Pennsylvania	Feb 1733	58v
411	DENNISON, William	John Taylor	Jamaica	Oct 1732	61
412	DENT, Robert	Peter Simpson	Maryland	2 Dec 1728	38v
413	DENTHWAITE, Richard	Peter Simpson	Jamaica	Dec 1731	55

414	DENTON, John	John Taylor	Jamaica	10 Oct 1726	27
415	DENTON, Robert	John Taylor	Pennsylvania	28 Aug 1727	29v
416	DE REPHERE, Emanuel	Peter Simpson	Maryland	12 Jan 1727	25
417	DETMETRUS, Edward	Samuel Gloynes	Virginia	4 Dec 1727	32
418	DEVEREUX, John	William Cash	Antigua	2 Dec 1728	38v
419	DICKINS, Edward	John Cooke	Pennsylvania	18 Apr 1726	25v
420	DICKINS, Henry	John Cooke	Pennsylvania	25 Aug 1725	20v
421	DICKINSON, James	John Ball	Jamaica	14 Oct 1728	36v
422	DINGLE, Samuel	Peter Simpson	MARYLAND	4 Dec 1727	31v
423	DIXON, Thomas	Peter Simpson	Maryland	5 Dec 1726	28v
424	DODD, Moses	John Taylor	Jamaica	22 Feb 1726	19v
425	DODDELL, Thomas	John Taylor	Jamaica	18 Apr 1726	26
426	DOHANNE, Tulup	James Gerald	Pennsylvania	25 Aug 1725	20v
427	DOLEMAN, Eleanor	Peter Simpson	Jamaica	Jan 1731	52v
428	DONALDSON, Henry	James Gerald	JAMAICA	20 Jul 1726	26v
429	DONALDSON, John	Richard Bateman	Maryland	22 Feb 1726	19
430	DONOVAN, Thomas	James Gerald	Maryland	Nov 1732	61
431	DORAN, Charles	John Ball	Jamaica	14 Oct 1728	36v
432	DOUGLAS, Richard	Samuel Gloynes	Jamaica	6 Dec 1725	24v
433	DOWLISS, John	James Gerald	Maryland	22 Feb 1726	19v
434	DOWNIE, John	Peter Simpson	Virginia	14 Oct 1728	37
435	DRACOFF, Ebenezer	John Taylor	Jamaica	5 Apr 1725	20
436	DRAPER, Edward	William Burge	Maryland	Nov 1732	61
437	DRYSDEALE, Hugh	John Taylor	Jamaica	25 Aug 1725	20v
438	DUBOIS, Samuel	Peter Simpson	Antigua	14 Oct 1728	36v
439	DUBRENIL, Christopher	James Gerald	Maryland	13 Jan 1726	19
440	DUCK, Mary	William Burge	Jamaica	Jan 1731	52
441	DUDING, John	Willliam Burge	Maryland	Mar 1733	59
442	DULLISON, John	Joseph Whilton	Antigua	13 Oct 1729	42
443	DULWIDINE(?), Charles	Joseph Whilton	Antigua	13 Oct 1729	42
444	DUNCOMB, William	William Burge	Jamaica	Jan 1731	52

445	DUNDASS, John	James Gerald	Antigua	7 Jul 1729	40v
446	DUNSBY, John	Neal MacNeal	Antigua	25 Aug 1729	41
447	DUNWICK, John	James Gerald	Maryland	10 Oct 1726	28
448	DURKIN, John	James Gerald	Antigua	3 Jun 1728	33v
449	DURRANCE, Samuel	John Cooke	Virginia	10 Oct 1726	28
450	DWYER, Thomas	James Gerald	Maryland	28 Feb 1727	25v
451	DYALL, John	John Taylor	JAMAICA	25 Aug 1725	20v
452	DYE, James	Richard Bateman	Maryland	22 Feb 1726	19

E

453	EAGLES, John	James Gerald	Maryland	14 Jan 1730	39
454	EARLE, Richard	Christopher Veale	Virginia	5 Apr 1725	20
455	EAST, John	Peter Simpson	Antigua	2 Dec 1728	38v
456	EATON, John	Neal MacNeal	Maryland	Jan 1732	57v
457	EATON, Margret	William Burge	Maryland	4 Dec 1727	31v
458	EATON, Thomas	Neal MacNeal	Pennsylvania	Feb 1733	59
459	EAVENS, James	John Ball	Jamaica	26 Feb 1729	33
460	EBERALL, John	Peter Simpson	MARYLAND	10 Apr 1727	29v
461	EBINSLLY, Thomas	John Williams	MARYLAND	Sep 1720	6
462	EBORN, John	James Gerald	Antigua	2 Dec 1728	38v
463	EBSWORTH, Thomas	Capt Robert North	MARYLAND	15 Jan 1729	32v
464	EDGE, Richard	John Taylor	Maryland	13 Jan 1726	17v
465	EDGERLEY, Catharine	John Ball	Pennsylvania	16 Oct 1727	30v
466	EDMUNDS, Hugh	John Cooke	Virginia	13 Jan 1726	18v
467	EDMUSTON, William	John Ball	Jamaica	14 Oct 1728	36v
468	EDWARDS, Charles	Richard Bateman	Jamaica	13 Jan 1726	17v
469	EDWARDS, John	James Gerald	Jamaica	5 Apr 1725	20
470	EDWARDS, John	James Gerald	Maryland	10 Oct 1726	28
471	EDWARDS, Thomas	John Cooke	Virginia	13 Jan 1726	18v
472	EDWARDS, Thomas	Richard White	Nevis	1 Dec 1729	42v
473	EGILTON, Mary	Magdelin Jones	PENNSYLVANIA	16 Oct 1727	31
474	ELLIS, Josiah	James Gerald	Pennsylvania	Jan 1733	58v
475	ELLIS, Samuel	John Taylor	Jamaica	5 Apr 1725	20
476	ELLISTONE, John	Peter Simpson	PENNSYLVANIA	23 May 1726	26v
477	ELWOOD, George	Peter Simpson	Maryland	Dec 1732	61v
478	EVANS, Jane	John Ball	Pennsylvania	16 Oct 1727	30v
479	EVANS, John	John Taylor	Jamaica	10 Oct 1726	27
480	EVINS, Edward	James Gerald	Maryland	4 Dec 1727	32

F

481	FAIRCLOUGH, Joseph	Capt Laborious Pearce	Pennsylvania	10 Oct 1726	28
482	FALLGATE, Israel	Richard Bateman	Jamaica	13 Jan 1726	17v
483	FARAN, Augustine	Peter Simpson	Jamaica	Jan 1731	52v
484	FARDWAL, Alexander	John Taylor	America	11 Jan 1728	29v
485	FARMER, William	John Ball	Antigua	2 Dec 1728	38
486	FARRANT, John	William Cash	Maryland	14 Oct 1728	37v
487	FARROW, John	William Burge	Antigua	14 Oct 1728	36
488	FAUSSETT, William	Neal MacNeal	Jamaica	Nov 1732	61
489	FERN, Francis	John Ball	Jamaica	14 Oct 1728	36v
490	FERRY, Daniel	John Cooke	Virginia	13 Jan 1726	18v
491	FERY, Thomas	John Taylor	Pennsylvania	28 Aug 1727	29v
492	FETTON, Randall	Neal MacNeal	Pennsylvania	Feb 1733	59
493	FIELD, William	Richard Bateman	Maryland	22 Feb 1726	19
494	FIELDER, Charles	John Taylor	Jamaica	Dec 1732	62
495	FIELDER, Martha	John Taylor	Jamaica	18 Apr 1726	26
496	FINCH, James	John Ball	Jamaica	26 Feb 1729	33
497	FINCH, John	John Cooke	Jamaica	9 Aug 1726	27
498	FITZHARRIS, John	James Gerald	Pennsylvania	25 Aug 1729	41
499	FLETCHER, Benjamin	Peter Simpson	Maryland	5 Dec 1726	28v
500	FLETCHER, Thomas	John Taylor	Jamaica	Aug 1730	43
501	FLETCHER, William	Peter Simpson	Jamaica	Dec 1731	55
502	FLINT, Richard	William Burge	Jamaica	Feb 1732	58
503	FLOYD, John	James Gerald	Maryland	14 Oct 1728	37v
504	FLOYD, John	Richard White	Antigua	13 Oct 1729	42
505	FLOYD, Robert	John Taylor	Barbados	14 Oct 1728	37
506	FLOWERS, William	James Gerald	Maryland	18 Apr 1726	26
507	FOGG, Edward	John Ball	Maryland	14 Oct 1728	37
508	FORBAS, John	John Taylor	Jamaica	Jan 1731	53
509	FORD, Christopher	John Dykes	Maryland	13 Jan 1726	17v
510	FORD, Thomas	John Taylor	Pennsylvania	28 Aug 1727	29v

511	FORRESTER, Rowland	John Taylor	Jamaica	5 Apr 1725	20
512	FORRIST, John	John Cooke	Jamaica	10 Oct 1726	27v
513	FOSTER, James	James Gerald	Antigua	2 Dec 1728	38v
514	FOSTER, John	Peter Simpson	Virginia	14 Oct 1728	37
515	FOSTER, Joseph	Neal MacNeal	Maryland	Dec 1732	61v
516	FOSTER, Thomas	William Burge	Antigua	14 Oct 1728	36
517	FOX, George	Robert Arbuthnot	ANTIGUA	Feb 1733	59
518	FOX, John	James Gerald	Maryland	13 Jan 1726	18v
519	FOX, Richard	Neal MacNeal	Jamaica	Jan 1733	58
520	FRANCIS, James	William Burge	VIRGINIA	26 Feb 1729	33
521	FRANCIS, John	James Gerald	Pennsylvania	18 Apr 1726	26v
522	FRANCIS, Thomas	Peter Simpson	Maryland	26 Feb 1729	32v
523	FRANCOIS, Lewis Charles	Richard Bateman	Maryland	22 Feb 1726	19
524	FREEGOOD, John	William Black	MARYLAND	22 Feb 1726	19v
525	FREEMAN, John	John Cooke	Jamaica	6 Dec 1725	24v
526	FRENCH, Francis	John Taylor	Pennsylvania	16 Oct 1727	30v
527	FRENCH, Samuel	Neal MacNeal	Jamaica	Nov 1732	61
528	FROST, Thomas	John Cooke	Pennsylvania	5 Apr 1725	20
529	FRUEN, John	Samuel Gloynes	Maryland	15 Jan 1729	32v
530	FULLER, Bartholomew	Richard White	Antigua	13 Oct 1729	42v
531	FULFORD, Fortunatus	William Burge	Antigua	14 Oct 1728	36
532	FULLFORD, John	Richard White	Nevis	1 Dec 1729	42v
533	FUNISY(?), Stephen	Joseph Whilton	Jamaica	14 Apr 1729	40
534	FYF, Robert	John Taylor	Jamaica	20 Jul 1726	26v

G

535	GALEY, John	Peter Simpson	Virginia	4 Dec 1727	32
536	GAMBELL, Robert	John Taylor	Jamaica	29 Apr 1728	33v
537	GARLER, James	Peter Simpson	Maryland	5 Dec 1726	28v
538	GARNACHON, Samuel	James Gerald	Antigua	Jan 1727	49v
539	GARNET, Robert	John Taylor	Maryland	6 Dec 1725	24v
540	GARNETT, Thomas	Neal MacNeal	Jamaica	19 May 1729	40v
541	GARON, David	John Ball	Pennsylvania	16 Oct 1727	30v
542	GASTINE, Jacob	Samuel Gloynes	Pennsylvania	18 Apr 1726	26
543	GATES, John	John Taylor	Pennsylvania	16 Oct 1727	30v
544	GAULLAIRD, John Peter	Christopher Veale	PENNSYLVANIA	15 Jan 1724	14
545	GAY, William Jnr	Neal MacNeal	Pennsylvania	Feb 1733	59
546	GEDDES, Robert	Peter Simpson	Antigua	2 Dec 1728	38v
547	GEEKIE, David	John Taylor	Jamaica	26 Feb 1729	33
548	GELSTRAP, Peter	John Taylor	Jamaica	10 Oct 1726	27
549	GHARRET, Thomas	John Cooke	Maryland	22 Feb 1726	19v
550	GIBBONS, William	John Ball	Pennsylvania	16 Oct 1727	30
551	GIBBS, John	William Cash	Jamaica	4 Jan 1730	39v
552	GIBSON, Mary	John Ball	Maryland	4 Dec 1727	31v
553	GIBSON, Robert	Peter Simpson	Pennsylvania	13 Oct 1729	41v
554	GILBERT, Edward	Peter Simpson	Maryland	5 Dec 1726	28v
555	GILBERT, Robert	James Gerald	Pennsylvania	18 Apr 1726	26v
556	GILFORD, John	Neal MacNeal	Pennsylvania	Feb 1733	59
557	GILKS, William	John Ball	Maryland	4 Dec 1727	31v
558	GILL, George	John Taylor	Jamaica	25 Aug 1725	20v
559	GILLBURD, Edward	John Taylor	Jamaica	15 Jan 1729	32v
560	GILLFORD, James	John Taylor	Jamaica	. Feb 1730	47v
561	GINN, Richard	Peter Simpson	Maryland	2 Dec 1728	38v
562	GLADIN, John	Richard Bateman	Maryland	22 Feb 1726	19
563	GLOVER, William	James Gerald	Jamaica	6 Dec 1725	24
564	GOAF(?), David	Joseph Whilton	Antigua	13 Oct 1729	42

565	GODBY, Sherlot Arabella	James Gerald	Virginia	5 Dec 1726	29
566	GODDARD, Mary	John Dykes	Pennsylvania	25 Aug 1725	21
567	GODWIN, William	James Gerald	Maryland	14 Jan 1730	39
568	GOFF, John	Peter Simpson	Maryland	Dec 1732	61v
569	GOFF, William	John Taylor	Jamaica	Dec 1732	62
570	GOIN, John	Bartholomew Voakes	N.D.	25 Aug 1725	20v
571	GOODWIN, John	John Taylor	Jamaica	9 Aug 1726	27
572	GORDEN, Roger	Neal MacNeal	Pennsylvania	Feb 1733	59
573	GOSSLING, Robert	William Burge	PENNSYLVANIA	28 Aug 1727	29v
574	GRAFON, Thomas	Peter Simpson	Maryland	Dec 1731	54v
575	GRAHAM, James	John Taylor	Jamaica	11 Oct 1725	21
576	GRAINGER, Caesar	John Taylor	Jamaica	Mar 1731	54
577	GRANT, Andrew	Neal MacNeal	Jamaica	Nov 1732	61
578	GRANT, Benjamin	John Ball	Jamaica	15 Jan 1729	32v
579	GRANT, Major	James Gerald	Pennsylvania	18 Apr 1726	26v
580	GRAVENER, Henry	John Taylor	Jamaica	13 Oct 1729	42
581	GRAY, Martin	Samuel Gloynes	Jamaica	16 Oct 1727	31
582	GRAY, Miles	Samuel Gloynes	Maryland	13 Jan 1726	17v
583	GRAY, Robert	John Taylor	Jamaica	2 Dec 1728	38
584	GREEN, Charles	John Cooke	Jamaica	5 Dec 1726	29
585	GREEN, William	Samuel Gloynes	Maryland	13 Jan 1726	17v
586	GREENWOOD, John	Samuel Gloynes	Maryland	13 Jan 1726	18
587	GREGG, Thomas	Neal MacNeal	Antigua	13 Oct 1729	41v
588	GREGG, William	Neal MacNeal	Maryland	Dec 1732	62
589	GRHIMS, Francis	Neal MacNeal	Jamaica	19 May 1729	40v
590	GRIFFIS, Thomas	John Taylor	Jamaica	Jan 1731	53
591	GRIMES, John	Peter Simpson	Maryland	14 Feb 1730	39v
592	GRIMMET, John	John Taylor	Jamaica	11 Oct 1725	21
593	GRIMSLY, Richard	John Taylor	Jamaica	19 May 1729	40
594	GRINSLADE, John	James Gerald	Pennsylvania	15 Jul 1728	35
595	GRON, Solomon	John Cooke	Jamaica	6 Dec 1725	24v

596	GUERIN, Peter	Richard Chapman	JAMAICA	18 Apr 1726	26
597	GULLYMORE, Matthew	John Taylor	Jamaica	2 Dec 1728	38
598	GURNEY, Robert	John Cooke	Jamaica	5 Dec 1726	29
599	GUTTERIDGE, Susanna	John Ball	Jamaica	14 Oct 1728	36v
600	GYLES, Jane	John Ball	Maryland	4 Dec 1727	31v

601	HALES, John	John Cooke	Virginia	13 Jan 1726	18
602	HALL, John	William Burge	Jamaica	Feb 1732	58
603	HALL, John	Neal MacNeal	Maryland	Dec 1732	62
604	HALL , Joseph	James Gerald	Antigua	2 Dec 1728	38v
605	HALL, Thomas	John Cooke	Jamaica	5 Dec 1726	29
606	HALL, Thomas	Joseph Whilton	Pennsylvania	13 Oct 1729	42
607	HALL, William	William Williams	SOUTH CAROLINA	28 Aug 1727	30
608	HALL, William	James Gerald	Maryland	4 Dec 1727	32
609	HALL, William	James Gerald	Pennsylvania	Jan 1733	58v
610	HALSTED, George	Peter Simpson	Jamaica	Dec 1731	55
611	HAMERTON, Thomas	John Ball	Maryland	4 Dec 1727	31v
612	HAMMERTON, George	Neal MacNeal	Maryland	Mar 1733	59v
613	HAMMOND, Anthony	James Gerald	Maryland	13 Jan 1726	18v
614	HAMMOND, John	Peter Simpson	PENNSYLVANIA	3 Jun 1728	33v
615	HAMOTT, John	Samuel Gloynes	Virginia	4 Dec 1727	32
616	HAMSON, Matthew	William Burge	Antigua	14 Oct 1728	37v
617	HANAWAY, Thomas	John Taylor	Jamaica	Jan 1733	58v
618	HANBEN, Christian	John Taylor	Jamaica	Jul 1732	60
619	HANCOCK, James	John Cooke	Maryland	11 Oct 1725	21
620	HANCOCK, Margret	John Cooke	Pennsylvania	5 Apr 1725	20
621	HANFORD, William	John Cooke	Virginia	13 Jan 1726	18v
622	HARBOY, Thomas	John Ball	Jamaica	26 Feb 1729	33
623	HARDING, James	John Taylor	New England	Nov 1732	61v
624	HARDING, Jesse	John Taylor	Jamaica	19 May 1729	40
625	HARDING, Rachael	Peter Simpson	Jamaica	Jan 1733	58v
626	HARDMAN, James	Peter Simpson	Maryland	14 Feb 1730	39v
627	HARDY, John	John Taylor	Jamaica	25 Aug 1725	20v
628	HARDY, Robert	Peter Simpson	Jamaica	Jan 1731	52v
629	HARE, Thomas	James Gerald	New England	Dec 1732	62
630	HARPER, William	Neal MacNeal	Jamaica	Jan 1733	58

631	HARRAP, Thomas	Neal MacNeal	Antigua	25 Aug 1729	41
632	HARRAWER, William	Joseph Whilton	Pennsylvania	13 Oct 1729	42
633	HARRIS, Edward	John Cooke	Virginia	10 Oct 1726	28
634	HARRIS, James	John Ball	Jamaica	14 Oct 1728	36v
635	HARRIS, John	Samuel Gloynes	Maryland	13 Jan 1726	18
636	HARRIS, John	Samuel Gloynes	Pennsylvania	18 Apr 1726	26
637	HARRIS, Joseph	Samuel Gloynes	Maryland	13 Jan 1726	18
638	HARRIS, Margret	James Gerald	Jamaica	5 Apr 1725	20
639	HARRIS, Richard	Peter Simpson	Maryland	5 Dec 1726	28v
640	HARRIS, Sacheverell	Peter Simpson	Pennsylvania	16 Oct 1727	31
641	HARRISON, Francis	John Taylor	Jamaica	Sep 1732	60v
642	HARRISON, George	Peter Simpson	Pennsylvania	13 Oct 1729	41v
643	HARRISON, John	Richard Bateman	MARYLAND	15 Jan 1724	14
644	HARRISON, William	James Gerald	New England	Dec 1732	62
645	HART, William	John Cooke	Maryland	22 Feb 1726	19v
646	HARVEY, John	William Cash	Jamaica	14 Apr 1729	40
647	HARVEY, Mary	James Towers	PENNSYLVANIA	10 Apr 1727	29v
648	HARWOOD, Robert	Samuel Gloynes	Maryland	13 Jan 1726	18
649	HASKETT, John	William Burge	MARYLAND	Oct 1732	60v
650	HASSER, Thomas	James Gerald	Pennsylvania	25 Aug 1725	21
651	HASSETT, Robert	James Gerald	Maryland	13 Jan 1726	19
652	HATCH, Purbeck	John Taylor	Pennsylvania	16 Oct 1727	30v
653	HATTEN, Hugh	John Taylor	America	Oct 1730	45
654	HAWEIS, William	Peter Simpson	Maryland	Dec 1731	54v
655	HAWES, John	Neal MacNeal	Jamaica	Jun 1732	60
656	HAWKES, John	John Taylor	Antigua	7 Jul 1729	40v
657	HAWKES, Smallecombe	James Gerald	Maryland	14 Oct 1728	37v
658	HAWKSWORTH, Thomas	Samuel Gloynes	Maryland	11 Jan 1728	29
659	HAYCRAFT, John	John Dykes	Maryland	11 Oct 1725	21v
660	HAYES, William	John Taylor	MARYLAND	15 Jan 1724	13v
661	HAYNES, John	William Burge	Antigua	14 Oct 1728	36

662	HAYNES, Samuel	James Gerald	Jamaica	14 Oct 1728	36v
663	HAYS, James	John Taylor	Pennsylvania	28 Aug 1727	29v
664	HAZELWOOD, Samuel	John Ball	Maryland	11 Jan 1728	29v
665	HEAD, John	John Taylor	Pennsylvania	16 Oct 1727	30v
666	HEADLEY, John	James Gerald	Jamaica	6 Dec 1725	24
667	HEATH, Gerrald	James Gerald	Maryland	18 Apr 1726	25v
668	HELLAM, Joseph	James Gerald	Jamaica	11 Oct 1725	21v
669	HELSBY, Richard	Alexander Cash	NEVIS	1 Dec 1729	42v
670	HENDERSON, Jane	Peter Simpson	Virginia	14 Oct 1728	37
671	HENNING, David	John Ball	Pennsylvania	16 Oct 1727	30v
672	HENSON, Benjamin	William Trottman	MARYLAND	Oct 1732	60v
673	HERBERT, Margret	John Ball	Maryland	4 Dec 1727	31v
674	HERBERT, Sarah	Peter Simpson	Barbados	Feb 1733	59
675	HERRING, Francis	Christopher Veale	PENNSYLVANIA	15 Jan 1724	14
676	HESS, Abraham	James Gerald	Jamaica	14 Oct 1728	36v
677	HEWISON, Thomas	William Burge	Maryland	Nov 1732	61
678	HICKMAN, James	Peter Simpson	Maryland	18 Apr 1726	26
679	HICKS, William	John Dykes	MARYLAND	6 Dec 1725	25
680	HIDE, Martha	John Ball	Antigua	2 Dec 1728	39
681	HIGGINS, John	Peter Simpson	Maryland	5 Dec 1726	28v
682	HILL, Robert	John Cooke	Jamaica	6 Dec 1725	24v
683	HILLIARD, Benjamin	John Ball	Pennsylvania	16 Oct 1727	30v
684	HILTON , John	William Cash	Virginia	6 Dec 1725	25
685	HINCHLEY, Samuel	James Gerald	Jamaica	5 Apr 1725	20
686	HINCK, William	John Ball	Maryland	14 Oct 1728	37
687	HOBBS, John	William Coleman	ST CHRISTOPHER	18 Apr 1726	26
688	HOBBS, Thomas	Samuel Farmer	MARYLAND	14 Jan 1730	39v
689	HOGG, John	James Gerald	Maryland	14 Jan 1730	39
690	HOGGELL, Robert	John Cooke	Pennsylvania	18 Apr 1726	26v
691	HOLDEN, Thomas	William Burge	Jamaica	14 Oct 1728	38
692	HOLDFORD, John	John Taylor	Jamaica	12 Jan 1727	25

- 693	HOLDSWORTH, Richard	Colo Charles Price	JAMAICA	10 Oct 1726	28
694	HOLDWAY, Philip	James Gerald	Maryland	10 Oct 1726	28
695	HOLEMARK, Thomas	Peter Simpson	Maryland	Mar 1733	59v
696	HOLFORD, John	William Burge	Virginia	16 Oct 1727	31
697	HOLFORD, Richard	Peter Simpson	Virginia	14 Oct 1728	37
698	HOLLAND, James	James Gerald	Pennsylvania	15 Jul 1728	35
699	HOLLENS, John	James Gerald	Maryland	14 Jan 1730	39
700	HOLLIER, William	Peter Simpson	New England	Nov 1732	61v
701	HOLLOWAY, James	Joseph Whilton	Pennsylvania	13 Oct 1729	42
702	HOLMES, John	Peter Simpson	Jamaica	Jul 1730	46v
703	HOLMES, Robert	Christopher Veale	PENNSYLVANIA	15 Jan 1724	14
704	HOLT, Emanuel	James Gerald	Maryland	13 Jan 1726	18v
705	HOLT, George	John Ball	Antigua	2 Dec 1728	38
706	HOMAN, Richard	Peter Simpson	Jamaica	1 Dec 1729	42v
707	HOPCRAFT, Thomas	James Gerald	Antigua	7 Jul 1729	40v
708	HOPE, William	Neal MacNeal	Jamaica	Aug 1732	60v
709	HOPKINS , Charles	John Taylor	Maryland	13 Jan 1726	17v
710	HOPKINS, John	John Cooke	Maryland	22 Feb 1726	19
711	HOPKINS, John	Richard White	Antigua	13 Oct 1729	42v
712	HOPSON, Samuel	John Ball	Maryland	29 Apr 1728	33v
713	HORNBY, William	Neal MacNeal	Jamaica	Jul 1732	60
714	HORNE, William	John Taylor	Jamaica	5 Apr 1725	19v
715	HOWARD, Eustice	John Taylor	Virginia or Jamaica	May 1720	5v
716	HOWARD, Joseph	James Gerald	Antigua	Jan 1727	49v
717	HOWARD, Thomas	James Gerald	JAMAICA	Apr 1732	59v
718	HOWARD, Thomas	Peter Simpson	Jamaica	Jan 1733	58v
719	HOWARD, William	John Taylor	Jamaica	Mar 1733	59v
720	HOWELL, Anthony	Peter Simpson	Maryland	Dec 1731	54v
721	HOWLAND, John	William Burge	Virginia	Dec 1732	62
722	HOWSE, Augustine	John Cooke	Jamaica	6 Dec 1725	24v

723	HUDSON, Andrew	William Cash	Maryland	14 Feb 1730	40
724	HUGHES, James	John Dykes	Maryland	11 Oct 1725	21v
725	HUGHES, John	Samuel Gloynes	PENNSYLVANIA	18 Apr 1726	26
726	HUGHES, John	Peter Simpson	Maryland	Dec 1731	54v
727	HUGHES, John	Neal MacNeal	Jamaica	Aug 1732	60v
728	HUGHES, Tobias	John Taylor	Jamaica	5 Apr 1725	20
729	HUGHS, Elizabeth	John Cooke	Pennsylvania	5 Apr 1725	20
730	HUMPHREYS, John	William Cash	Antigua	26 Aug 1728	35v
731	HUNT, John	John Ball	Jamaica	14 Oct 1728	36v
732	HUNTER, Abraham	Neal MacNeal	Antigua	13 Oct 1729	41v
733	HUNTER, David	James Gerald	Pennsylvania	25 Aug 1729	41
734	HUNTER, John	Christopher Veale	MARYLAND	15 Jan 1724	14
735	HURCOM, Thomas	Richard White	Nevis	1 Dec 1729	42v
736	HURLEY, William	Samuel Gloynes	Jamaica	6 Dec 1725	24v
737	HURLY, James	Samuel Gloynes	Virginia	4 Dec 1727	32
738	HUSBAND, Robert	John Taylor	Pennsylvania	15 Jul 1728	35
739	HUSON, Francis	James Gerald	Maryland	13 Jan 1726	19
740	HUSSEY, Peter	Neal MacNeal	Jamaica	Nov 1732	61
741	HUTCHESON, Alexander	John Taylor	Jamaica	26 Feb 1729	33
742	HUTCHINS, Joseph	John Taylor	Jamaica	25 Aug 1729	41
743	HUTCHINSON, Charles	William Burge	Jamaica	Feb 1732	58
744	HUTCHINSON, James	James Gerald	Jamaica	5 Apr 1725	20
745	HUTT, Charles	James Gerald	Jamaica	6 Dec 1725	23v
746	HUTTON, Joshua	William Cash	Maryland	14 Oct 1728	37v
747	HUTTON, John	Edward Perry	JAMAICA	Feb 1732	58
748	HUXLEY, John	Richard Bateman	Maryland	6 Dec 1725	25

I

749	IBINSON, Thomas	James Gerald	Antigua	Jan 1727	49ν
750	IBISON, William	Peter Simpson	Maryland	Dec 1731	54ν
751	INGLETON, Christopher	William Burge	Maryland	14 Feb 1730	40
752	IRELAND, Arthur	Neal MacNeal	Jamaica	Nov 1732	61

J

753	JACKSON, John	James Gerald	Pennsylvania	25 Aug 1725	21
754	JAKES, Richard	John Taylor	Jamaica	Sep 1732	60v
755	JAMES, Elisha	John Cooke	Virginia	13 Jan 1726	18
756	JAMES, Francis	James Gerald	Virginia	5 Dec 1726	28v
757	JAMES, John	James Gerald	ANTIGUA	15 Jan 1724	14
758	JAMES, John	Neal MacNeal	Maryland	Dec 1732	61v
759	JAMES, Thomas	Samuel Gloynes	Maryland	13 Jan 1726	18
760	JANDSON, William	John Taylor	Pennsylvania	15 Jul 1728	35
761	JARVIS, John	William Cash	Maryland	14 Oct 1728	37v
762	JARVIS, Richard	John Cooke	Maryland	22 Feb 1726	19
763	JEFFERSON, John	John Taylor	Jamaica	22 Feb 1726	19v
764	JENKINS, Even	James Gerald	Jamaica	6 Dec 1725	23v
765	JENKINS, Susannah	Peter Simpson	Maryland	14 Jan 1730	39v
766	JENKINSON, Jacob	John Dykes	Pennsylvania	25 Aug 1725	21
767	JEPSON, John	Peter Simpson	Pennsylvania	13 Oct 1729	41v
768	JEWSON, Joseph	John Ball	Pennsylvania	16 Oct 1727	30v
769	JINNINGS, Sarah	James Gerald	Jamaica	11 Oct 1725	21v
770	JOHNSON, John	Richard Bateman	Jamaica	13 Jan 1726	17v
771	JOHNSON, John	William Cash	Jamaica	14 Apr 1729	40
772	JOHNSON, Nathaniel	Peter Simpson	Maryland	5 Dec 1726	28v
773	JOHNSON, Paul	William Burge	Pennsylvania	29 Apr 1728	33v
774	JOHNSON, William	John Taylor	Jamaica	2 Dec 1728	38
775	JOHNSON, William	Peter Simpson	Maryland	14 Jan 1730	39v
776	JOLLIFE, John	John Ball	Antigua	2 Dec 1728	38
777	JONES, Bridgett	John Ball	Maryland	4 Dec 1727	31v
778	JONES, Henry	John Taylor	Jamaica	25 Aug 1729	41
779	JONES, Hugh	John Taylor	Maryland	6 Dec 1725	24v
780	JONES, John	John Cooke	Virginia	13 Jan 1726	18
781	JONES, John	William Williams	SOUTH CAROLINA	28 Aug 1727	30
782	JONES, John	John Ball	Pennsylvania	16 Oct 1727	30

783	JONES, John	John Taylor	JAMAICA	1 Dec 1729	42v
784	JONES, John	James Gerald	Maryland	Nov 1732	61
785	JONES, Jonathan	John Ball	Jamaica	26 Feb 1729	33
786	JONES, Joseph	John Ball	Jamaica	14 Oct 1728	36v
787	JONES, Mary	Neal MacNeal	Jamaica	Jul 1732	60
788	JONES, Richard	John Taylor	Jamaica	2 Dec 1728	38
789	JONES, Richard	William Cash	Maryland	15 Jan 1729	32v
790	JONES, Simon	John Ball	Jamaica	14 Oct 1728	36v
791	JONES, Thomas	James Gerald	Virginia	5 Dec 1726	28v
792	JONES, Thomas	John Ball	Maryland	29 Apr 1728	33v
793	JONES, Thomas	John Ball	Jamaica	26 Feb 1729	33
794	JONES, William	Neal MacNeal	Jamaica	Jan 1733	58
795	JORDAN, Ann	Peter Simpson	Virginia	14 Oct 1728	37
796	JORDAN, Joshua	James Gerald	JAMAICA	May 1732	59v
797	JOSEPH, Edward	Neal MacNeal	Maryland	Dec 1732	61v
798	JOYCE, John	James Gerald	Jamaica	6 Dec 1725	23v
799	JUB, John	John Taylor	South Carolina	May 1732	60
800	JULL, Thomas	John Cooke	Jamaica	6 Dec 1725	24v

K

801	KEATHRAN, Richard	Neal MacNeal	Jamaica		Sep 1732	60v
802	KELLY, Thomas	John Ball	VIRGINIA	16 Oct 1727	30
803	KELSHER, John	James Gerald	Maryland	10 Oct 1726	28
804	KENDALL, Joseph	James Gerald	Jamaica	10 Oct 1726	27v
805	KENNON, Samuel	John Weasenham	Maryland or Virginia		May 1720	5v
806	KER, Thomas	James Gerald	Maryland	10 Oct 1726	28
807	KESTINE, Stephen	John Ball	Antigua	2 Dec 1728	38
808	KEY, James	John Cooke	Jamaica	6 Dec 1725	24v
809	KEYMER, William	John Taylor	Maryland	6 Dec 1725	25
810	KEYS, William	John Cooke	Jamaica	6 Dec 1725	24v
811	KEYS, William	John Taylor	Jamaica	14 Oct 1728	37v
812	KIDWELL, Charles	Samuel Gloynes	Jamaica	5 Apr 1725	19v
813	KING, Henry	John Taylor	New England		Nov 1732	61v
814	KING, James	John Taylor	Maryland	10 Oct 1726	27v
815	KING, Nicholas	Samuel Gloynes	Jamaica	6 Dec 1725	24
816	KING, Richard	John Taylor	Jamaica	15 Jan 1729	32v
817	KING, Roderick	James Gerald	Barbados	20 Jul 1726	26v
818	KING, William	John Taylor	Jamaica	10 Oct 1726	27
819	KINNICK, Robert	Samuel Gloynes	Maryland	11 Jan 1728	29
820	KIRBY, James	Peter Simpson	Maryland	14 Feb 1730	39v
821	KITCHIN, Francis	William Cash	Maryland	14 Oct 1728	37v
822	KLUCK, Anne	John Taylor	Jamaica		Oct 1732	61
823	KNAPP, Henry	John Cooke	Virginia	13 Jan 1726	18v
824	KNIGHT, Thomas	John Ball	Antigua	2 Dec 1728	39
825	KNIGHT, William	Peter Simpson	Maryland		Mar 1733	59v
826	KNOTT, John	John Ball	Maryland	11 Jan 1728	29v
827	KNOWLES, Stephen	Neal MacNeal	Antigua	13 Oct 1729	41v

L

828	LADLEY, James	John Taylor	Jamaica	7 Jul 1729	40v
829	LAFENDE, Walter	John Taylor	Jamaica	26 Feb 1729	33v
830	LAFEVER, John	John Cooke	Jamaica	10 Oct 1726	27v
831	LAHY, Nicholas	Richard Bateman	JAMAICA	5 Apr 1725	19v
832	LAKEWARD, Thomas	Samuel Gloynes	Jamaica	6 Dec 1725	24
833	LAMAR, Abraham	James Gerald	Jamaica	14 Oct 1728	36v
834	LAMBURN, John	John Cooke	Virginia	13 Jan 1726	18
835	LAMING, Marshall	James Gerald	Maryland	10 Oct 1726	28
836	LANG, Laurance	John Cooke	Jamaica	10 Oct 1726	27v
837	LANGFORD, Benjamin	John Taylor	Jamaica	20 Jul 1726	26v
838	LAREMAR, Elizabeth	John Cooke	Pennsylvania	18 Apr 1726	26v
839	LA ROCHE, Mary Ann	William Burge	Jamaica	14 Oct 1728	38
840	LASH, Philip	John Ball	Jamaica	14 Oct 1728	36v
841	LAW, John	Peter Simpson	Maryland	10 Oct 1726	28
842	LAWRANCE, William	Samuel Gloynes	Jamaica	16 Oct 1727	31
843	LAWRENCE, Isaac John	Peter Simpson	Pennsylvania	13 Oct 1729	41v
844	LAWRENCE, Robert	Peter Simpson	Maryland	14 Feb 1730	39v
845	LAWSON, John	James Gerald	Virginia	5 Dec 1726	29
846	LAXTON, Matthew	John Taylor	Jamaica	18 Apr 1726	26
847	LAY, Abraham	John Cooke	Jamaica	5 Dec 1726	29
848	LAY, Richard	John Ball	Pennsylvania	16 Oct 1727	30
849	LEARWOOD, Paul	John Taylor	Maryland	13 Jan 1726	17v
850	LEE, John	Peter Simpson	Maryland	18 Apr 1726	26
851	LEE, Peter	John Taylor	Jamaica	23 May 1726	26v
852	LEE, Samuel	John Taylor	Jamaica	5 Dec 1726	29
853	LEE, Thomas	John Ball	Jamaica	26 Feb 1729	33
854	LEGGETT, John	John Cooke	Jamaica	9 Aug 1726	26v
855	LEIVES, William	John Taylor	Jamaica	Jul 1732	60
856	LELLO, John	Neal MacNeal	Maryland	Dec 1732	62
857	LEONARD, Edward	William Cash	Maryland	14 Oct 1728	37v

858	LEPPER, Robert	John Cooke	Virginia	13 Jan 1726	18v
859	LEWIS, George	James Gerald	Jamaica	6 Dec 1725	24
860	LEWIS, Hugh	William Burge	Antigua	14 Oct 1728	37v
861	LEWIS, Joseph	John Cooke	Virginia	10 Oct 1726	28
862	LEWIS, William	John Taylor	Jamaica	Dec 1732	62
863	LIDDERDALE, Francis	John Taylor	Jamaica	12 Jan 1727	25
864	LIGHT, Thomas	Peter Simpson	Antigua	2 Dec 1728	38v
865	LIGHTBOWN, Thomas	John Cooke	Pennsylvania	18 Apr 1726	25v
866	LIGHTWOOD, John	John Ball	Maryland	14 Oct 1728	37
867	LIMBER, Thomas	John Dykes	Pennsylvania	25 Aug 1725	21
868	LINCOLN, Paul	Peter Simpson	Pennsylvania	13 Oct 1729	41v
869	LINDSEY, David	Peter Simpson	Virginia	14 Oct 1728	37
870	LLOYD, David	James Gerald	Jamaica	14 Oct 1728	36v
871	LLOYD, Robert	William Burge	Pennsylvania	29 Apr 1728	33v
872	LLOYD, Thomas	John Taylor	Jamaica	25 Aug 1729	41
873	LOCKYEE, Thomas	John Cooke	Jamaica	6 Dec 1725	24v
874	LOMAX, John	John Dykes	Maryland	13 Jan 1726	17v
875	LONGSTAFF, George	James Gerald	Jamaica	14 Oct 1728	36v
876	LOWRY, John	William Cash	Virginia	6 Dec 1725	25
877	LUCAS, Ann	John Cooke	Pennsylvania	18 Apr 1726	25v
878	LUCAS, James	Peter Simpson	Jamaica	Jul 1732	60
879	LUDIMAN, John	John Cooke	Jamaica	10 Oct 1726	27v
880	LUKE, William	James Gerald	Virginia	5 Dec 1726	29
881	LUNSON, Thomas	Peter Simpson	New England	Nov 1732	61v

M

882	MACHIN, William	Peter Simpson	New England	Nov 1732	61v
883	MACGHIE, Alexander	James Gerald	Antigua	7 Jul 1729	40v
884	MACKAY, John	John Cooke	Jamaica	10 Oct 1726	27v
885	MACKPHERSON, Alexander	John Taylor	Jamaica	Jan 1731	53
886	MADDOX, Benjamin	Richard Bateman	Maryland	22 Feb 1726	19
887	MAER, William	William Burge	Virginia	14 Apr 1729	40
888	MAHOON, Lewis	Neal MacNeal	Jamaica	Jul 1732	60
889	MAIE, George	John Taylor	Pennsylvania	15 Jul 1728	35
890	MAKEPEACE, William	Tobias Bowles	MARYLAND	11 Oct 1725	21
891	MALLET, Ephrahim	James Gerald	Jamaica	6 Dec 1725	24
892	MAN, Samuel	James Gerald	Pennsylvania	25 Aug 1729	41
893	MAN, Thomas	Samuel Gloynes	Maryland	13 Jan 1726	18
894	MANLY, Charles	John Taylor	Jamaica	Feb 1733	59
895	MANNING, Richard	Christopher Veale	MARYLAND	15 Jan 1724	14
896	MANSFIELD, John	John Taylor	Jamaica	15 Jan 1729	32v
897	MANSFIELD, Richard	James Gerald	Pennsylvania	25 Aug 1725	20v
898	MARK, Peter	John Johnson	N.D.	13 Oct 1718	2
899	MARKLIN, John	William Trottman	Pennsylvania	Feb 1733	59
900	MARLEY, John	Richard White	Maryland	14 Feb 1730	39v
901	MARLOW, William	John Taylor	Pennsylvania	16 Oct 1727	30v
902	MARNER, John	William Burge	JAMAICA	Aug 1732	60v
903	MARSHALL, John	James Gerald	Jamaica	6 Dec 1725	24
904	MARSHALL, Richard	John Taylor	Jamaica	Oct 1732	61
905	MARSHALL, Robert	James Gerald	Jamaica	6 Dec 1725	23v
906	MARSHALL, Samuel	John Taylor	Jamaica	14 Oct 1728	37v
907	MARTEN, Richard	John Cooke	Jamaica	5 Dec 1726	29
908	MARTIN, Jesper	James Gerald	Jamaica	16 Oct 1727	31
909	MARTIN, Mathew	John Taylor	South Carolina	May 1732	60
910	MASCALL, Robert	Peter Simpson	Maryland	15 Jan 1729	32v
911	MASON, John	Richard Bateman	Maryland	22 Feb 1726	19

912	MASON, John	Neal MacNeal	Maryland	Dec 1732	62
913	MASON, William	Samuel Gloynes	Pennsylvania	18 Apr 1726	26
914	MASON, William	Peter Simpson	Maryland	5 Dec 1726	29
915	MASSAM, Richard	Peter Simpson	Pennsylvania	13 Oct 1729	41v
916	MASTION, Francis	John Taylor	South Carolina	Mar 1732	58
917	MATHEW, James	Peter Simpson	Virginia	14 Oct 1728	37
918	MATHEWS, William	John Taylor	Jamaica	Jul 1732	60
919	MATHEWS, William	James Gerald	Pennsylvania	Jan 1733	58v
920	MAUDE, James	Samuel Gloynes	Jamaica	6 Dec 1725	24
921	MAXFIELD, Henry	John Taylor	Barbados	14 Oct 1728	37
922	MAXWELL, James	Samuel Gloynes	Jamaica	6 Dec 1725	24
923	MAY, James	Christopher Veale	NORTH CAROLINA	15 Jan 1724	14
924	MAYLIEGH, Richard Blancourt	Elias Booth	VIRGINIA	10 Oct 1726	27v
925	MAYNE, Luke	James Gerald	Jamaica	14 Oct 1728	36v
926	MAYO, Joseph	Samuel Gloynes	Jamaica	6 Dec 1725	24
927	MAYSTON, Robert	John Taylor	Jamaica	Jun 1732	60
928	MCKAY, Andrew	John Taylor	Barbados	14 Oct 1728	37
929	MEAKES, Thomas	James Gerald	JAMAICA	19 May 1729	40v
930	MEDLE, Charles	James Gerald	Pennsylvania	15 Jul 1728	35
931	MEDLEY, James	James Gerald	Jamaica	6 Dec 1725	23v
932	MEEKS, George	James Gerald	Maryland	4 Dec 1727	32
933	MEERS, Richard	James Gerald	Jamaica	14 Oct 1728	36v
934	MELLIN, James	William Cash	Antigua	26 Aug 1728	35v
935	MEREDITH, Thomas	William Burge	MARYLAND	Jan 1733	58v
936	MERRYMAN, Joseph	John Taylor	Jamaica	15 Jan 1729	32v
937	METCALFE, Leonard	William Williams	SOUTH CAROLINA	28 Aug 1727	30
938	MIDDLETON, John	John Taylor	New England	Nov 1732	61v
939	MIDDLETON, Simon	Christopher Veale	MARYLAND	15 Jan 1724	14
940	MIDDLETON, William	Peter Simpson	Maryland	15 Jan 1729	32v
941	MIHILL, Samuel	William Burge	Antigua	14 Oct 1728	36
942	MILES, Jeffery	John Taylor	Jamaica	5 Apr 1725	19v

943	MILES, John	Peter Simpson	Maryland	14 Jan 1730	39v
944	MILLER, Baptist	John Cooke	Jamaica	6 Dec 1725	24v
945	MILLER, James	John Ball	Jamaica	26 Feb 1729	33
946	MINIKING, Thomas	Richard White	Antigua	13 Oct 1729	42
947	MINTO, Walter	James Gerald	Jamaica	15 Jan 1729	32v
948	MITTAULT, Francis	James Gerald	Jamaica	6 Dec 1725	23v
949	M'LACLAN, Robert	John Gregory	Jamaica	5 Dec 1726	28
950	MONROE, Daniel	James Gerald	Maryland	4 Dec 1727	32
951	MOONE, William	Peter Simpson	Pennsylvania	16 Oct 1727	31
952	MOORE, Daniel	Neal MacNeal	Pennsylvania	14 Apr 1729	40
953	MOORE, Dennis	Peter Simpson	Maryland	Jan 1727	49
954	MOORE, Job	John Cooke	Virginia	13 Jan 1726	18
955	MOORE, John	William Burge	PENNSYLVANIA	15 Jan 1729	32v
956	MOORE, Samuel	Neal MacNeal	Maryland	Mar 1733	59v
957	MOORE, Thomas	James Gerald	Pennsylvania	25 Aug 1725	21
958	MOORE, Thomas	John Taylor	Jamaica	Nov 1729	48v
959	MOORE, William	Samuel Gloynes	Maryland	13 Jan 1726	18
960	MOORE, William	John Taylor	Antigua	13 Oct 1729	42
961	MOORE, William	William Trottman	Pennsylvania	Feb 1733	59
962	MORAN, Robert	Neal MacNeal	Virginia	14 Apr 1729	40
963	MORGAN, Evan	John Taylor	JAMAICA	18 Apr 1724	15v
964	MORGAN, Mercer	William Burge	Antigua	2 Dec 1728	38v
965	MORGAN, Samuel	John Taylor	Jamaica	13 Oct 1729	42
966	MORGETRYT, Elizabeth	James Gerald	Jamaica	11 Oct 1725	21v
967	MORGIN, John	John Taylor	Maryland	5 Dec 1726	28v
968	MORGIN, Thomas	John Cooke	Jamaica	6 Dec 1725	24v
969	MORLESS, Richard	Richard White	Nevis	1 Dec 1729	42v
970	MORLEY, George	James Gerald	Maryland	10 Oct 1726	28
971	MORLEY, William	Neal MacNeal	Antigua	13 Oct 1729	41v
972	MORRIS, Henry	John Taylor	Jamaica	Oct 1732	61
973	MORRIS, John	John Cooke	Virginia	13 Jan 1726	18v

974	MORRIS, Mary	John Cooke	Pennsylvania	18 Apr 1726	25v
975	MORRIS, Samuel	Samuel Gloynes	MARYLAND	26 Feb 1729	33
976	MORRIS, Valentine	Peter Simpson	Virginia	14 Oct 1728	37
977	MORRIS, Thomas	James Gerald	Pennsylvania	25 Aug 1725	20v
978	MORRIS, William	James Gerald	Maryland	28 Feb 1727	25v
979	MORRISSON, Peter	John Taylor	Jamaica	26 Feb 1729	33v
980	MORTIMER, Alexander	John Dykes	Maryland	11 Oct 1725	21v
981	MORTOE, William	James Gerald	Maryland	Nov 1732	61
982	MORTON, William	John Cooke	Virginia	10 Oct 1726	28
983	MOSES, John	James Gerald	Pennsylvania	25 Aug 1725	21
984	MOULDER, Thomas	John Taylor	Maryland	13 Jan 1726	17v
985	MOULDING, Edward	Peter Simpson	Maryland	14 Jan 1730	39v
986	MUMFORD, Patiance	Samuel Gloynes	Virginia	4 Dec 1727	32
987	MURPHY, William	Capt Thomas Annis	PENNSYLVANIA	18 Apr 1726	26
988	MURRAY, James	Elias Booth	VIRGINIA	10 Oct 1726	27v
989	MURRAY, William	John Taylor	Jamaica	14 Oct 1728	37v
990	MURREY, John	William Cash	Virginia	11 Oct 1725	21v
991	MURROE, Elias	John Taylor	Jamaica	18 Apr 1726	26

N

992	NARWOOD, Richard	William Burge	Maryland	Nov 1732	61
993	NASH, Partrick	Neal MacNeal	Jamaica	Nov 1732	61
994	NEALL, William	James Gerald	Pennsylvania	25 Aug 1725	21
995	NELSON, George	James Gerald	Barbados	20 Jul 1726	26v
996	NETHERWAY, Thomas	John Taylor	Jamaica	13 Oct 1729	42
997	NEVILL, Ann	John Ball	Pennsylvania	16 Oct 1727	30v
998	NEVILL, John	William Burge	Virginia	16 Oct 1727	31
999	NEVILL, John	Neal MacNeal	MARYLAND	Apr 1732	59v
1000	NEWBELL, William	James Gerald	Maryland	13 Jan 1726	18v
1001	NEWCOMB, Edward	John Taylor	South Carolina	May 1732	60
1002	NEWELL, William	John Cooke	Virginia	20 Jul 1726	26v
1003	NEWEY, Simon	John Taylor	Jamaica	28 Feb 1727	25v
1004	NEWLAND, Thomas	James Gerald	Jamaica	Jan 1731	49v
1005	NEWMAN, Henry	Richard White	Maryland	14 Feb 1730	39v
1006	NEWSTEAD, Joseph	John Taylor	Jamaica	Dec 1732	62
1007	NEWSTEAD, Thomas	James Gerald	Pennsylvania	Jan 1733	58v
1008	NEWTON, Edward	Joseph Whilton	Antigua	13 Oct 1729	42
1009	NEWTON, Samuel	John Ball	Maryland	14 Oct 1728	37
1010	NEWTON, Thomas	John Cooke	Jamaica	9 Aug 1726	27
1011	NICHOLLS, John	Joseph Whilton	Pennsylvania	29 Apr 1728	33v
1012	NICHOLLS, Michael Howell	John Dykes	Maryland	11 Oct 1725	21v
1013	NICHOLLS, Michael	Richard White	Nevis	1 Dec 1729	42v
1014	NICHOLLS, Robert	William Burge	Antigua	13 Oct 1729	41v
1015	NICKELLS, James	Neal MacNeal	Jamaica	19 May 1729	40v
1016	NIMMO, John	Samuel Gloynes	MARYLAND	10 Apr 1727	29v
1017	NOBLE, John	Peter Simpson	New England	Nov 1732	61v
1018	NOBLE, Robert	Neal MacNeal	Maryland	Jan 1732	57v
1019	NORMAN, Anthony	James Gerald	Pennsylvania	15 Jul 1728	35
1020	NORMAN, Thomas	Peter Simpson	Virginia	4 Dec 1727	32
1021	NORTON, Samuel	William Burge	Pennsylvania	29 Apr 1728	33v

| 1022 | NORTON, William | William Cash | Antigua | 2 Dec 1728 | 38v |
| 1023 | NOYELL, Daniel | James Gerald | JAMAICA | Jun 1732 | 60 |

O

1024	ODELL, William	Peter Simpson	Antigua	14 Oct 1728	36v
1025	ODLING, John	Neal MacNeal	Jamaica	Jun 1732	60
1026	OKEY, William	James Gerald	Maryland	28 Feb 1727	25v
1027	OLIVER, John	Richard White	Antigua	13 Oct 1729	42
1028	O'RAILEY, Peter	Joseph Whilton	Jamaica	7 Jul 1729	40v
1029	ORAM, Catharine	Samuel Gloynes	Jamaica	16 Oct 1727	31
1030	ORRELL, Ralph	Richard Bateman	Maryland	22 Feb 1726	19
1031	OSBORN, Richard	John Taylor	Jamaica	14 Apr 1729	40
1032	OSBORNE, Edward	John Cooke	Jamaica	10 Oct 1726	27v
1033	OSBORNE, John	Neal MacNeal	Jamaica	May 1732	59v
1034	OSBORNE, William	John Taylor	Jamaica	Dec 1732	62
1035	OSBOURNE, William	Richard White	Maryland	14 Feb 1730	39v
1036	OUNSWORTH, Richard	Samuel Gloynes	Maryland	15 Jan 1729	32v
1037	OURSLERE, Edward	James Gerald	Jamaica	5 Apr 1725	20
1038	OWEN, Matthew	John Cooke	Maryland	22 Feb 1726	19
1039	OWEN, Thomas	William Cash	Maryland	14 Oct 1728	37v
1040	OWEN, William	John Taylor	Pennsylvania	15 Jul 1728	35
1041	OXMAN, Mary	William Cash	Maryland	14 Oct 1728	37v

P

1042	PAGE, Daniel	William Burge	Pennsylvania	29 Apr 1728	33v
1043	PAGE, Mary	John Cooke	Pennsylvania	18 Apr 1726	25v
1044	PAINTER, Samuel	Neal MacNeal	Maryland	Dec 1732	62
1045	PAIST, Charles	John Taylor	Pennsylvania	16 Oct 1727	30v
1046	PALMER, Isabela	Peter Simpson	Jamaica	Aug 1732	60v
1047	PALMER, William	Peter Simpson	Maryland	5 Dec 1726	28v
1048	PARIS, Germain	Neal MacNeal	Jamaica	7 Jul 1729	40v
1049	PARKER, Joseph	Samuel Gloynes	Maryland	13 Jan 1726	18
1050	PARKER, Richard	John Cooke	Maryland	11 Oct 1725	21
1051	PARKER, William	Capt Robert North	MARYLAND	15 Jan 1729	32v
1052	PARR, Samuel	James Gerald	Pennsylvania	25 Aug 1725	20v
1053	PARRIS, Thomas	Samuel Gloynes	Virginia	4 Dec 1727	32
1054	PARRISH, Richard	John Cooke	Jamaica	9 Aug 1726	27
1055	PARROCK, Francis	John Cooke	Jamaica	10 Oct 1726	27v
1056	PARSONS, Henry	John Cooke	VIRGINIA	5 Apr 1725	20
1057	PARTON, Abraham	Peter Simpson	MARYLAND	10 Apr 1727	29v
1058	PASHELL, Gamchiel	William Cash	Maryland	26 Feb 1729	32v
1059	PATILLO, John	James Gerald	Maryland	4 Dec 1727	32
1060	PATRICKS, Robert	James Gerald	Pennsylvania	25 Aug 1725	21
1061	PATY, James	Samuel Gloynes	Maryland	2 Dec 1728	38v
1062	PAYNE, George	Neal MacNeal	Jamaica	Jan 1733	58
1063	PAYNE, John	John Taylor	Maryland or Pennsylvania	May 1720	5v
1064	PEACOCK, Clement	Peter Simpson	Maryland	14 Jan 1730	39v
1065	PEARCE, James	Peter Simpson	Antigua	14 Oct 1728	36v
1066	PEARCY, Eleanor	John Ball	Pennsylvania	16 Oct 1727	30v
1067	PEARSE, William	Richard Bateman	Maryland	22 Feb 1726	19
1068	PEARSON, John	John Taylor	Antigua	26 Aug 1728	36
1069	PEARSON, William	John Ball	Maryland	14 Oct 1728	37
1070	PEATER, Richard	Richard Bateman	Maryland	6 Dec 1725	25

1071	PEBWORTH, William	James Gerald	Maryland	14 Oct 1728	37v
1072	PEDDER, Joseph	James Gerald	Pennsylvania	Feb 1733	58v
1073	PEKINS, John	John Taylor	Jamaica	Jan 1731	53
1074	PENNELL, John	Thomas Nickson	MARYLAND	22 Feb 1726	19v
1075	PENNOCK, Joseph	John Taylor	Jamaica	Mar 1733	59v
1076	PENNY, John	Neal MacNeal	Maryland	Dec 1732	62
1077	PEPLOW, John	William Cash	Maryland	15 Jan 1729	32v
1078	PERRIN, John	Peter Simpson	Maryland	Dec 1732	61v
1079	PERRY, Hugh	Peter Simpson	MARYLAND	11 Jan 1728	29
1080	PERRY, William	James Gerald	Virginia	5 Dec 1726	28v
1081	PETERS, John	James Gerald	Pennsylvania	15 Jul 1728	35
1082	PETERS, William	Samuel Gloynes	Maryland	13 Jan 1726	17v
1083	PETERSON, Francis	Peter Simpson	Jamaica	Dec 1731	55
1084	PETLEY, Thomas	John Taylor	Jamaica	12 Jan 1727	25
1085	PETTEY, Thomas	John Cooke	Virginia	20 Jul 1726	26v
1086	PEW, John	John Taylor	Jamaica	2 Dec 1728	38
1087	PEW, Robert	John Ball	Jamaica	26 Feb 1729	33
1088	PHELPS, John	Joseph Whilton	Antigua	13 Oct 1729	42
1089	PHILLIP, George	John Cooke	Jamaica	10 Oct 1726	27
1090	PHILLIPS, Ann	James Gerald	Jamaica	11 Oct 1725	21v
1091	PHILLIPS, John	John Cooke	PENNSYLVANIA	23 May 1726	26v
1092	PHILLIPS, Nichollas	Richard Bateman	Maryland	22 Feb 1726	19
1093	PHILLIPS, Richard	John Taylor	Jamaica	Jan 1731	53
1094	PHIPPS, Thomas	Neal MacNeal	Jamaica	Jan 1733	58
1095	PICARD, Abell	John Cooke	Virginia	13 Jan 1726	18
1096	PICKERSGILL, John	James Gerald	Maryland	10 Oct 1726	28
1097	PICKHAVER, Thomas	John Ball	Jamaica	26 Feb 1729	33
1098	PICKTON, William	Peter Simpson	Maryland	15 Jan 1729	32v
1099	PIKES, Thomas	Richard White	Antigua	13 Oct 1729	42
1100	PIMLOT, William	John Cooke	Virginia	13 Jan 1726	18
1101	PIPER, Thomas	John Cooke	Jamaica	10 Oct 1726	27v

1102	PITCHER, Abraham	John Taylor	Jamaica	7 Jul 1729	40v
1103	PITCHFORD, Samuel	John Cooke	Jamaica	6 Dec 1725	24v
1104	PITTS, Thomas	James Gerald	Pennsylvania	Jan 1732	57v
1105	PLATT, Cornelius	Peter Simpson	Maryland	28 Feb 1727	25v
1106	PLIMLY, Samuel	John Taylor	Jamaica	18 Apr 1726	26
1107	POGCON, John	John Taylor	Barbados	14 Oct 1728	37
1108	POLHILL, Robert	Neal MacNeal	Pennsylvania	Feb 1733	59
1109	PONT, Henry	Peter Simpson	Maryland	10 Oct 1726	27v
1110	POPE, Timothy	Thomas Nickson	MARYLAND	22 Feb 1726	19v
1111	PORTER, James	James Gerald	VIRGINIA	1721	8
1112	PORTER, John	John Dykes	SOUTH CAROLINA	15 Jan 1724	14v
1113	PORTER, Matthew	John Taylor	Jamaica	2 Dec 1728	38
1114	POTTER, Samuel	John Taylor	Jamaica	4 Dec 1727	31
1115	POWELL, Charles	James Gerald	Virginia	5 Dec 1726	28v
1116	POWELL, Evan	James Gerald	Jamaica	11 Oct 1725	21v
1117	POWELL, James	William Burge	Jamaica	Jan 1731	52
1118	POWELL, John	Thomas Nixson	Maryland	Jan 1732	57v
1119	POWELL, Richard	James Gerald	Maryland	13 Jan 1726	18v
1120	POWELL, Richard	John Taylor	Jamaica	26 Feb 1729	33
1121	PRAT, Thomas	John Taylor	Jamaica	19 May 1729	40
1122	PRATT, Thomas	Peter Simpson	Maryland	Dec 1731	54v
1123	PRATTEN, Joseph	Richard Bateman	Maryland	6 Dec 1725	25
1124	PRENTICE, John	Samuel Gloynes	Maryland	26 Feb 1726	19v
1125	PRENTICE, Thomas	James Gerald	Maryland	Nov 1732	61
1126	PRESTON, Edward	John Cooke	Virginia	13 Jan 1726	18
1127	PRICE, David	Richard Bateman	JAMAICA	18 Apr 1726	26
1128	PRICE, John	John Cooke	Virginia	13 Jan 1726	18
1129	PRICE, John	John Cooke	Jamaica	10 Oct 1726	27v
1130	PRICE, Lewis	James Gerald	Jamaica	1721	8
1131	PRICE, Philip	John Taylor	Jamaica	10 Oct 1726	27
1132	PRICE, Richard	Richard White	Maryland	14 Feb 1730	39v

1133	PRICE, Thomas	John Taylor	Jamaica	5 Apr 1725	19v
1134	PRICE, William	Richard White	Nevis	1 Dec 1729	42v
1135	PRIEST, William	William Cash	Pennsylvania	13 Oct 1729	41
1136	PRITCHETT, John	Neal MacNeal	Maryland	Mar 1733	59v
1137	PRITTY, Jacob	John Taylor	Maryland	10 Oct 1726	27v
1138	PROCTER, William	James Gerald	Jamaica	26 Feb 1729	33
1139	PULLIN, William	John Ball	Jamaica	14 Oct 1728	36v
1140	PULLMAN, Mary	Peter Simpson	Jamaica	Jan 1733	58v
1141	PURY, Peter	William Burge	Virginia	Dec 1732	62
1142	PYE, Edward	Neal MacNeal	Jamaica	Jan 1733	58

Q

| 1143 | QUARY, John | John Ball | Jamaica | 15 Jan 1729 | 32v |
| 1144 | QUICK, Samuel | William Burge | Jamaica | Feb 1731 | 54 |

R

1145	RAMM, John	John Cooke	Virginia	13 Jan 1726	18
1146	RANDALL, Henry	James Gerald	Maryland	11 Jan 1728	29v
1147	RANDALL, Robert	William Cash	Jamaica	4 Jan 1730	39v
1148	RANDS, John	John Cooke	Pennsylvania	18 Apr 1726	25v
1149	RANEW, John	John Cooke	Pennsylvania	18 Apr 1726	25v
1150	RANSOM, John	Neal MacNeal	Jamaica	Jul 1730	46v
1151	RAWLINS, John	Richard Bateman	Jamaica	13 Jan 1726	17v
1152	RAWLINS, John	Peter Simpson	Jamaica	10 Oct 1726	27v
1153	RAWLINSON, Mary	John Dykes	Pennsylvania	25 Aug 1725	21
1154	RAWSON, William	John Ball	Antigua	2 Dec 1728	39
1155	RAY, Thomas	Richard White	Nevis	1 Dec 1729	42v
1156	RAYMOND, James	Richard Bateman	Maryland	22 Feb 1726	19
1157	RAYMOND, Thomas	William Burge	Barbados	Mar 1732	58
1158	RAYNALDS, Thomas	Peter Simpson	Jamaica	Jul 1732	60
1159	READ, Abigall	Peter Simpson	Maryland	5 Dec 1726	29
1160	READ, John.	Peter Simpson	Maryland	Jan 1727	49
1161	READ, William	John Taylor	Jamaica	Jan 1731	53
1162	REDMAN, John	John Cooke	Pennsylvania	18 Apr 1726	26
1163	REDMAYNE, Christopher	Peter Simpson	Maryland	15 Jan 1729	32v
1164	REDMUND, Jeremiah	Samuel Gloynes	Jamaica	6 Dec 1725	24
1165	REEVE, Benjamin	Samuel Gloynes	Maryland	22 Feb 1726	19v
1166	REMINGTON, John	James Gerald	Jamaica	26 Feb 1729	33
1167	REYNALDS, Thomas	John Taylor	Pennsylvania	16 Oct 1727	30v
1168	REYNOLDS, Elizabeth	John Cooke	Pennsylvania	18 Apr 1726	25v
1169	RHODES, Robert	John Taylor	Jamaica	23 May 1726	26v
1170	RICE, William	Peter Simpson	Maryland	Jan 1727	49
1171	RICHARDSON, George	James Gerald	Maryland	10 Oct 1726	28
1172	RICHARDSON, John	Joseph Whilton	Jamaica	7 Jun 1729	40v
1173	RICHARDSON, Thomas	John Cooke	Pennsylvania	18 Apr 1726	25v
1174	RICHIE, Patrick	John Ball	Maryland	14 Oct 1728	37

1175	RIDLE, Richardson	Christopher Veale	MARYLAND	15 Jan 1724	14
1176	RIDLEY, William	John Taylor	Jamaica	Feb 1732	58
1177	RIDOUT, William	Peter Simpson	Maryland	Dec 1732	61v
1178	ROBERTS, James	Neal MacNeal	Antigua	13 Oct 1729	41v
1179	ROBERTS, Joseph	John Cooke	Jamaica	9 Aug 1726	27
1180	ROBERTS, Mary	Peter Simpson	Maryland	12 Jan 1727	25
1181	ROBERTS, Matthew	John Cooke	Jamaica	9 Aug 1726	26v
1182	ROBINSON, James	James Gerald	MARYLAND	25 Aug 1725	20v
1183	ROBINSON, James	John Taylor	Jamaica	14 Oct 1728	37v
1184	ROBINSON, John	Peter Simpson	Maryland	Mar 1733	59v
1185	ROBINSON, Robert	Neal MacNeal	Maryland	Dec 1732	62
1186	ROBINSON, Thomas	Capt Laborious Pearce	PENNSYLVANIA	10 Oct 1726	28
1187	ROBINSON, William	James Gerald	Maryland	13 Jan 1726	18v
1188	ROE, Michael	Peter Simpson	Barbados	Feb 1733	59
1189	ROEBUCK, Edward	Neal MacNeal	Jamaica	Mar 1732	58
1190	ROGERS, John	John Cooke	Pennsylvania	18 Apr 1726	25v
1191	ROGERS, John	John Taylor	Jamaica	10 Oct 1726	27
1192	ROOT, William	James Gerald	Maryland	28 Feb 1727	25v
1193	ROPER, Thomas	John Ball	Pennsylvania	16 Oct 1727	30v
1194	ROSE, William	Peter Simpson	Maryland	Dec 1731	54v
1195	ROUNTREE, Richard	James Gerald	Maryland	10 Oct 1726	28
1196	ROUSE, William	Peter Simpson	Maryland	5 Dec 1726	29
1197	ROWSE, Zacharias	James Gerald	Maryland	10 Oct 1726	28
1198	ROWSWELL, Samuel	John Dykes	Pennsylvania	25 Aug 1725	21
1199	ROY, Alexander	Peter Simpson	Jamaica	18 Apr 1726	26v
1200	RUDD, Thomas	Peter Simpson	Virginia	14 Oct 1728	37
1201	RUMBALL, Richard	Samuel Gloynes	Virginia	4 Dec 1727	32
1202	RUSSELL, Henry	Peter Simpson	Maryland	14 Feb 1730	39v
1203	RUSSELL, John	John Cooke	Jamaica	5 Dec 1726	29
1204	RUTHORN, Thomas	John Taylor	Jamaica	22 Feb 1726	19v
1205	RYEBUTT, Joseph	James Gerald	Jamaica	6 Dec 1725	24

| 1206 | RYE, Anthony | John Dykes | Maryland | 13 Jan 1726 | 17v |
| 1207 | RYLES, William | Neal MacNeal | Jamaica | Mar 1732 | 58 |

S

1208	SADLER, John	John Taylor	Jamaica	11 Oct 1725	21
1209	SAGE, Henry	Peter Simpson	Jamaica	Jan 1733	58v
1210	SAINT CLARE , John	Peter Simpson	Maryland	12 Jan 1727	25
1211	SAKRENS, Edward	John Ball	Antigua	2 Dec 1728	38
1212	SALISBURY, Richard	William Burge	Antigua	14 Oct 1728	36
1213	SARNDERS, Thomas	John Taylor	VIRGINIA OR JAMAICA	May 1720	5v
1214	SATCHWELL, Joseph	Peter Simpson	Maryland	Dec 1731	54v
1215	SAVIDGE, Thomas	Neal MacNeal	Jamaica	Jan 1733	58
1216	SAYWELL, Lydia	Samuel Gloynes	Virginia	4 Dec 1727	32
1217	SCORYER, Richard	James Gerald	Virginia	5 Dec 1726	29
1218	SCOTT, George	James Gerald	Pennsylvania	Jan 1733	58v
1219	SCOTT, John	Neal MacNeal	Maryland	Dec 1732	62
1220	SCOTT, Martin	Neal Martin	Antigua	13 Oct 1729	41v
1221	SCOTT, Samuel	Peter Simpson	Maryland	Dec 1732	61v
1222	SCRIVENER, Benjamin	Joseph Whilton	Pennsylvania	13 Oct 1729	42
1223	SEAGER, Peter	James Gerald	Maryland	13 Jan 1726	18v
1224	SEARCH, Christopher	James Gerald	Maryland	14 Oct 1728	37v
1225	SEARSE, William	John Taylor	Jamaica	11 Oct 1725	21
1226	SEBIRE, John Jnr	William Burge	Antigua	13 Oct 1729	41v
1227	SEDDON, Samuel	James Gerald	Maryland	Nov 1732	61
1228	SENNER, Cary	John Taylor	Jamaica	Dec 1732	62
1229	SERGENT, James	James Gerald	Maryland	13 Jan 1726	19
1230	SETTERINGTON, James	Peter Simpson	Jamaica	May 1732	59v
1231	SEVEER, Abraham	Peter Simpson	Antigua	14 Oct 1728	36v
1232	SEYMOUR, William	Henry Griffith	JAMAICA	10 Oct 1726	27v
1233	SHAW, Oliver	Peter Simpson	Maryland	28 Feb 1727	25v
1234	SHEPPARD, Charles	Peter Simpson	New England	Nov 1732	61v
1235	SHEPPARD, John	James Gerald	Maryland	13 Jan 1726	18v
1236	SHEPPARD, Thomas	John Taylor	Jamaica	13 Oct 1729	42

1237	SILDSLY, George	John Taylor	Jamaica	5 Apr 1725	20
1238	SILVERSIDE, Isaac	Peter Simpson	Jamaica	Aug 1732	60v
1239	SILVESTER, John	Francis Blane	Pennsylvania	14 Apr 1729	40
1240	SIME, William	William Cash	Antigua	2 Dec 1728	38v
1241	SIMMONS, Thomas	William Cash	Jamaica	19 May 1729	40v
1242	SIMONS, Elizabeth	Peter Simpson	Maryland	5 Dec 1726	28v
1243	SIMPSON, Benjamin	Peter Simpson	Maryland	Jan 1727	49
1244	SIMPSON, James	Peter Simpson	Jamaica	Jul 1732	60
1245	SIMPSON, John	John Ball	Jamaica	26 Feb 1729	33
1246	SIMPSON, Samuel	John Taylor	Jamaica	25 Aug 1725	20v
1247	SKEATS, John	James Gerald	Maryland	13 Jan 1726	18v
1248	SKELTON, John	John Taylor	Pennsylvania	16 Oct 1727	30v
1249	SKIPERTON, Francis	John Taylor	Jamaica	19 May 1729	40
1250	SLADE, Abraham	John Taylor	Jamaica	12 Jan 1727	25
1251	SMALL, Richard	Peter Simpson	Barbados	Feb 1733	59
1252	SMART, Thomas	James Gerald	Virginia	5 Dec 1726	28v
1253	SMITH, Daniel	William Cash	Pennsylvania	13 Oct 1729	41
1254	SMITH, James	John Cooke	Jamaica	9 Aug 1726	27
1255	SMITH, James	John Taylor	Jamaica	Oct 1732	61
1256	SMITH, John	William Chambers	JAMAICA	5 Dec 1726	28
1257	SMITH, John	John Taylor	Jamaica	29 Apr 1728	33v
1258	SMITH, John	John Taylor	Jamaica	14 Oct 1728	37v
1259	SMITH, John	William Cash	Jamaica	19 May 1729	40v
1260	SMITH, John	Neal MacNeal	Jamaica	Sep 1732	60v
1261	SMITH, John	William Burge	JAMAICA	Sep 1732	60v
1262	SMITH, Joseph	James Gerald	Maryland	13 Jan 1726	18v
1263	SMITH, Joseph	James Gerald	Virginia	5 Dec 1726	28v
1264	SMITH, Richard	John Cooke	Virginia	10 Oct 1726	28
1265	SMITH, Richard	Samuel Gloynes	Maryland	11 Jan 1728	29
1266	SMITH, Sarah	John Ball	Pennsylvania	16 Oct 1727	30v
1267	SMITH, Stephen	James Gerald	Maryland	22 Feb 1726	19v

1268	SMITH, Thomas	William Cash	Jamaica	19 May 1729	40v
1269	SMITH, Thomas	Neal MacNeal	Antigua	13 Oct 1729	42
1270	SMITH, Thomas	Neal MacNeal	Jamaica	May 1732	59v
1271	SMITH, William	Peter Simpson	Maryland	10 Oct 1726	27v
1272	SMITH, William	John Taylor	Jamaica	12 Jan 1727	25
1273	SMITH, William	William Burge	Antigua	14 Oct 1728	36
1274	SMITH, William	John Taylor	Jamaica	2 Dec 1728	38
1275	SMITH, William	William Burge	MARYLAND	Feb 1733	59
1276	SMITH, William	Samuel Gloynes	Maryland	2 Dec 1728	38v
1277	SMITH, William	Neal MacNeal	Maryland	Mar 1733	59v
1278	SMOUT, Timothy	Neal MacNeal	Maryland	Dec 1732	62
1279	SNAPE, Thomas	John Cooke	Maryland	5 Dec 1726	28v
1280	SNOULTEN, John	Richard White	Nevis	1 Dec 1729	42v
1281	SNOWDEN, Richard	John Cooke	Virginia	10 Oct 1726	28
1282	SOUTH, John	Bartholomew Voakes	N.D.	25 Aug 1725	20v
1283	SPEAK, Joseph	James Gerald	Maryland	28 Feb 1727	25v
1284	SPENCE, John	John Cooke	Jamaica	6 Dec 1725	24v
1285	SPENCE, Thomas	Peter Simpson	Antigua	14 Oct 1728	36v
1286	SPENCER, John	Richard Bateman	Jamaica	13 Jan 1726	17v
1287	SPRATT, William	Neal MacNeal	Antigua	13 Oct 1729	41v
1288	SPRINGFIELD, William	John Ball	Antigua	2 Dec 1728	38
1289	SPRINGULL, Jonathan	John Taylor	Jamaica	26 Feb 1729	33v
1290	STACKHOUSE, John	John Taylor	Jamaica	15 Jan 1729	32v
1291	STAKERS, Hugh	William Trottman	JAMAICA	Jan 1733	58v
1292	STAMPER, Charles	John Cooke	Jamaica	10 Oct 1726	27
1293	STANFORD, Luke	Neal MacNeal	Antigua	13 Oct 1729	41v
1294	STANLEY, John	James Gerald	Jamaica	14 Oct 1728	37
1295	STEAD, Richard	Peter Simpson	Maryland	10 Oct 1726	28
1296	STEED, Rebecca	Richard Bateman	Jamaica	13 Jan 1726	17v
1297	STEEL, Richard	John Taylor	Jamaica	15 Jan 1729	32v
1298	STEERE, Thomas	James Gerald	Jamaica	10 Oct 1726	27v

1299	STEPHENS, Joseph	John Taylor	Jamaica	Mar 1731	54
1300	STEPHENS, Richard	Richard Bateman	Maryland	6 Dec 1725	25
1301	STEPHENS, Thomas	Henry Griffith	JAMAICA	10 Oct 1726	27v
1302	STEPHENSON, Thomas	Peter Simpson	Jamaica	1 Dec 1729	42v
1303	STEVENS, John	John Taylor	Pennsylvania	28 Aug 1727	29v
1304	STEVENS, Robert	John Taylor	Jamaica	22 Feb 1726	19v
1305	STEVENS, Thomas	Peter Simpson	Virginia	4 Dec 1727	32
1306	STEVENSON, John	Peter Simpson	Maryland	14 Jan 1730	39v
1307	STEVENSON, Richard	John Taylor	Jamaica	14 Oct 1728	37v
1308	STEWARD, Charles	William Burge	Maryland	14 Feb 1730	40
1309	STEWARD, John	William Burge	Maryland	14 Feb 1730	40
1310	STEWARD, Robert	Neal MacNeal	Maryland	Mar 1733	59v
1311	STEWART, Alexander	John Cooke	Maryland	22 Feb 1726	19v
1312	STEWART, Charles	John Taylor	Jamaica	5 Dec 1726	29
1313	STEWART, James	James Gerald	Jamaica	6 Dec 1725	24
1314	STILES, James	Neal MacNeal	Jamaica	Nov 1732	61
1315	STILES, John	Neal MacNeal	Jamaica	Jul 1732	60
1316	STIRRUP, Robert	Richard Bateman	JAMAICA	18 Apr 1726	26
1317	STOKER, Henry	Peter Simpson	Maryland	Dec 1731	54v
1318	STOKES, Amas	John Taylor	Maryland	5 Dec 1726	28v
1319	STORER, John	John Taylor	Jamaica	23 May 1726	26v
1320	STREET, Samuel	John Cooke	Maryland	28 Feb 1727	25v
1321	STRINGER, Francis	James Gerald	JAMAICA	Aug 1732	60v
1322	STRONG, Nathaniel	Neal MacNeal	Maryland	14 Jan 1730	39v
1323	STROUD, John	John Taylor	Jamaica	14 Oct 1728	37v
1324	STUART, Joseph	Peter Simpson	Maryland	Dec 1732	61v
1325	STUART, Walter	Peter Simpson	Antigua	2 Dec 1728	38v
1326	STUD, Robert	Christopher Veale	MARYLAND	15 Jan 1724	14
1327	STYLES, Joseph	John Taylor	Jamaica	5 Apr 1725	20
1328	SUGG, Henry	John Taylor	Jamaica	7 Jul 1729	40v
1329	SULEWEN, Daniel	James Gerald	Maryland	4 Dec 1727	32

1330	SUMMERFIELD, Samuel	Peter Simpson	Pennsylvania	13 Oct 1729	41v
1331	SUMMERS, Thomas	Samuel Gloynes	Jamaica	6 Dec 1725	24
1332	SUMMERTON, John	Neal MacNeal	Maryland	Jan 1732	57v
1333	SUMMERWELL, William	John Dykes	Maryland	11 Oct 1725	21v
1334	SWAN, John	Richard White	Maryland	14 Feb 1730	39v
1335	SWAN, Sarah	John Taylor	Pennsylvania	28 Aug 1727	29v
1336	SWINDEN, George	John Ball	Antigua	2 Dec 1728	38

T

1337	TAGG, Edward	Neal MacNeal	Pennsylvania	Feb 1733	59
1338	TALBUTT, Jacob	Richard Bateman	Maryland	22 Feb 1726	19
1339	TANNIER, James	Peter Simpson	Antigua	2 Dec 1728	38v
1340	TAYLER, Cornish	John Taylor	Jamaica	5 Apr 1725	20
1341	TAYLER, Edward	John Cooke	Jamaica	6 Dec 1725	24v
1342	TAYLER, John	Joseph Whilton	Pennsylvania	29 Apr 1728	33v
1343	TAYLER, Patrick	John Gregory	JAMAICA	13 Jan 1726	17v
1344	TAYLER, Robert	James Gerald	Jamaica	12 Jan 1727	25
1345	TAYLER, Thomas	John Taylor	Jamaica	13 Oct 1729	42
1346	TAYLOR, David	John Taylor	Jamaica	Jan 1731	53
1347	TAYLOR, Richard	John Dykes	Pennsylvania	25 Aug 1725	21
1348	TAYLOR, William	Neal MacNeal	Jamaica	Jan 1733	58
1349	TEASDALE, George	John Taylor	Maryland	6 Dec 1725	24v
1350	TELLEY, Richard	John Ball	Jamaica	15 Jan 1729	32v
1351	TEMPLE, Ann	Richard Bateman	Jamaica	13 Jan 1726	17v
1352	TENNANT, William	John Ball	Jamaica	14 Oct 1728	36v
1353	TERRY, John	James Gerald	Jamaica	26 Feb 1729	33
1354	TEST, Joseph	William Burge	Virginia	16 Oct 1727	31
1355	TEVIODALE, Alexander	John Taylor	Jamaica	13 Oct 1729	42
1356	THOMAS, David	Peter Simpson	Jamaica	10 Oct 1726	27v
1357	THOMAS, George	Neal MacNeal	JAMAICA	Apr 1731	55v
1358	THOMAS, John	Peter Simpson	Maryland	Jan 1727	49
1359	THOMAS, Nathaniel	William Cash	Antigua	2 Dec 1728	38v
1360	THOMAS, Rice	James Gerald	Jamaica	15 Jan 1729	32v
1361	THOMAS, Robert	James Gerald	Maryland	22 Feb 1726	19v
1362	THOMAS, Robert	James Gerald	Pennsylvania	Feb 1733	58v
1363	THOMAS, William	John Cooke	Virginia	10 Oct 1726	28
1364	THOMAS, William	Capt Robert North	MARYLAND	15 Jan 1729	32v
1365	THOMPSON, John	John Taylor	Maryland	6 Dec 1725	24v
1366	THOMPSON, Methuselah	William Cash	Maryland	14 Feb 1730	40

1367	THOMPSON, Richard	Neal MacNeal	Jamaica	Sep 1732	60v
1368	THOMPSON, Thomas	John Dykes	VIRGINIA	May 1720	5v
1369	THORLEY, William	John Taylor	Jamaica	14 Apr 1729	40
1370	THORN, Richard	James Gerald	Pennsylvania	15 Jul 1728	35
1371	THRUP, Sarah	Peter Simpson	Maryland	5 Dec 1726	29
1372	TICEALL, Mary	Samuel Gloynes	Jamaica	16 Oct 1727	31
1373	TIFFIN, James	John Cooke	Jamaica	6 Dec 1725	24v
1374	TILLY, Edward	John Taylor	Jamaica	2 Aug 1725	20v
1375	TILLY, Thomas	John Cooke	Virginia	10 Oct 1726	28
1376	TIMS, George	Humphry Bell	VIRGINIA	Jan 1732	57v
1377	TOLLETT, Francis	William Burge	Maryland	Apr 1731	50
1378	TOOLE, Garret	Christopher Veale	MARYLAND	15 Jan 1724	14
1379	TOYNTON, Richard	John Taylor	Jamaica	Dec 1732	62
1380	TREHEARN, James	John Taylor	Maryland	6 Dec 1725	24v
1381	TREPLAND, James	James Gerald	Jamaica	6 Dec 1725	24
1382	TRESBY, John	John Cooke	Virginia	13 Jan 1726	18
1383	TREVERS, Thomas	Neal MacNeal	Jamaica	Oct 1732	60v
1384	TRISP, William	John Taylor	Jamaica	13 Oct 1729	42
1385	TUCKER, John	William Cash	Antigua	2 Dec 1728	38v
1386	TURNER, Edward	Neal MacNeal	Jamaica	Oct 1732	60v
1387	TURNER, John	James Gerald	Jamaica	6 Dec 1725	24
1388	TURNER, John	James Gerald	Maryland	4 Dec 1727	32
1389	TURNER, Michael	William Cash	Maryland	14 Oct 1728	37v
1390	TURNER, Nathaniel	Samuel Gloynes	Jamaica	16 Oct 1727	31
1391	TURNER, William	John Taylor	Pennsylvania	16 Oct 1727	30v
1392	TURNER, William	James Gerald	Maryland	Nov 1732	61
1393	TWIGGER, John	James Gerald	Jamaica	6 Dec 1725	23v
1394	TWISS, Humphrey	John Taylor	Pennsylvania	15 Jul 1728	35
1395	TWYCROSS, John	Neal MacNeal	Maryland	Mar 1733	59v
1396	TYLEE, John	John Cooke	Maryland	28 Feb 1727	25v

U

1397	UNCKLES, John	Peter Simpson	Maryland	5 Dec 1726	28v
1398	UNDAY, William	James Gerald	Jamaica	6 Dec 1725	23v
1399	UPHMORE, Richard	John Cooke	Jamaica	6 Dec 1725	24v
1400	UPTON, Thomas	Neal MacNeal	Maryland	Mar 1733	59v

V

1401	VANDERY, James	Neal MacNeal	Maryland	14 Jan 1730	39v
1402	VAUGHAN, John	Peter Simpson	Antigua	2 Dec 1728	38v
1403	VAUGHAN, John	John Taylor	Jamaica	26 Feb 1729	33
1404	VARY, Cornelius	Richard Bateman	Jamaica	13 Jan 1726	17v
1405	VINCENT, Blaze	Thomas Nixson	Maryland	Jan 1732	57v
1406	VINCENT, John	Richard Bateman	MARYLAND	15 Jan 1724	14
1407	VOCKINS, Hopefull	Neal MacNeal	Pennsylvania	29 Apr 1728	33v
1408	VOSS, George	James Gerald	Jamaica	5 Apr 1725	20

W

1409	WAGSTAFF, Joseph	Peter Simpson	Barbados	Feb 1733	59
1410	WAKEMAN, Theodorus	John Taylor	Jamaica	5 Apr 1725	20
1411	WALDEN, Emmanuel	William Burge	Pennsylvania	29 Apr 1728	33v
1412	WALDON, Henry	Peter Simpson	Maryland	14 Jan 1730	39v
1413	WALE, George	Peter Simpson	Maryland	Dec 1731	54v
1414	WALKER, Elizabeth	Peter Simpson	Pennsylvania	18 Apr 1726	26v
1415	WALKER, Jeffery	James Gerald	Antigua	7 Jul 1729	40v
1416	WALKER, Thomas	William Burge	Antigua	13 Oct 1729	41v
1417	WALKER, Thomas	Peter Simpson	Maryland	Mar 1733	59v
1418	WALLDEN, Richard	John Taylor	Maryland	13 Jan 1726	17v
1419	WALLER, John	James Gerald	New England	Dec 1732	62
1420	WALLIS, Alexander	John Dykes	Maryland	13 Jan 1726	17v
1421	WALLIS, Robert	John Dykes	MARYLAND	15 Jan 1724	14
1422	WAMSLEY, James	William Trottman	New England	Dec 1732	62
1423	WANN, Edward	John Taylor	Jamaica	5 Apr 1725	20
1424	WANN, Edward	James Gerald	Pennsylvania	25 Aug 1725	21
1425	WARD, Christopher	William Burge	Virginia	Dec 1732	62
1426	WARD, James	James Gerald	Jamaica	6 Dec 1725	24
1427	WARD, James	Joseph Whilton	Pennsylvania	13 Oct 1729	42
1428	WARD, Samuel	Samuel Gloynes	Virginia	4 Dec 1727	32
1429	WARE, Richard	Samuel Gloynes	Maryland	2 Dec 1728	38v
1430	WARE, Thomas	Peter Simpson	Maryland	Dec 1732	61v
1431	WARRIN, Martha	William Burge	MARYLAND	4 Dec 1727	32
1432	WASH, Joseph	Peter Simpson	Maryland	14 Jan 1730	39v
1433	WASHINGTON, William	Neal MacNeal	Jamaica	Oct 1732	60v
1434	WATERS, John	John Taylor	Jamaica	25 Aug 1729	41
1435	WATKINS, Rice	James Gerald	MARYLAND	18 Apr 1724	15v
1436	WATKINS, Samuel	Richard Bateman	MARYLAND	15 Jan 1724	14
1437	WATSON, James	Richard White	MARYLAND	14 Jan 1730	39
1438	WATSON, John	John Cooke	Jamaica	6 Dec 1725	24v

1439	WATSON, Thomas	Peter Simpson	Jamaica	Jun 1732	60
1440	WATSON, William	Samuel Gloynes	Maryland	13 Jan 1726	18
1441	WATSON, William	Neal MacNeal	Jamaica	May 1732	59v
1442	WAY, Ambrose	Neal MacNeal	Jamaica	Nov 1732	61
1443	WEALE, John	James Gerald	Antigua	3 Jun 1728	33v
1444	WEALE, John	John Taylor	Pennsylvania	15 Jul 1728	35
1445	WEAVER, Francis	John Cooke	Jamaica	9 Aug 1726	26v
1446	WEBB, George	James Gerald	Pennsylvania	18 Apr 1726	26v
1447	WEBB, Mark	Samuel Gloynes	Virginia	4 Dec 1727	32
1448	WEBBER, William	John Taylor	Jamaica	Feb 1733	59
1449	WEED, Robert	John Dykes	Pennsylvania	25 Aug 1725	21
1450	WEEDIN, Thomas	John Dykes	Maryland	13 Jan 1726	17v
1451	WELCH, Edward	William Cash	Maryland	14 Oct 1728	37v
1452	WELLFARE, Judeth	Peter Simpson	JAMAICA	Mar 1727	49v
1453	WELLING, William	John Cooke	Maryland	22 Feb 1726	19v
1454	WELSH, Robert	James Gerald	Jamaica	6 Dec 1725	23v
1455	WELSH, Thomas	John Ball	Pennsylvania	16 Oct 1727	30v
1456	WEST, Thomas	Jonathan Forward	VIRGINIA	Feb 1733	59
1457	WESTCOMBE, Samuel	Samuel Gloynes	Maryland	13 Jan 1726	18
1458	WETHERILL, Thomas	James Gerald	Pennsylvania	Jan 1733	58v
1459	WHALEY, James	Peter Simpson	Maryland	Dec 1731	54v
1460	WHEATLEY, Hugh	John Taylor	Jamaica	5 Apr 1725	20
1461	WHEATLEY, John	James Gerald	Jamaica	6 Dec 1725	23v
1462	WHEETLY, James	James Gerald	Maryland	4 Dec 1727	32
1463	WHITAKER, Samuel	John Taylor	Jamaica	5 Dec 1726	29
1464	WHITBEY, John	John Taylor	Jamaica	Jan 1731	53
1465	WHITE, David	Neal MacNeal	Virginia	14 Apr 1729	40
1466	WHITE, Elizabeth	William Cash	Virginia	11 Oct 1725	21v
1467	WHITE, George	Samuel Gloynes	Maryland	13 Jan 1726	18
1468	WHITE, James	Neal MacNeal	Maryland	Mar 1733	59v
1469	WHITE, John	Peter Simpson	Maryland	2 Dec 1728	38v

1470	WHITE, Thomas	John Cooke	Virginia	20 Jul 1726	26v
1471	WHITE, Ward	John Taylor	Jamaica	Jun 1732	60
1472	WHITEHEAD, Robert	John Taylor	Jamaica	13 Oct 1729	42
1473	WHITEHOUSE, Richard	William Burge	Jamaica	Jan 1731	52
1474	WHITHAM, Joseph	John Ball	Jamaica	26 Feb 1729	33
1475	WHITMAN, William	James Gerald	Pennsylvania	25 Aug 1725	21
1476	WHITTAKER, John	John Ball	Jamaica	26 Feb 1729	33
1477	WHITTERENCE, Lidia	William Cash	Maryland	1 Dec 1729	42v
1478	WHITTIN, Michael	Christopher Veale	VIRGINIA	May 1720	5v
1479	WHITTINGHAM, William	James Gerald	Jamaica	14 Oct 1728	37
1480	WHYLEY, Jonathan	James Gerald	Jamaica	6 Dec 1725	23v
1481	WICKES, Nehemiah	Isaac Stiff	JAMAICA	Jan 1731	53
1482	WICKSON, William	Joseph Whilton	Pennsylvania	26 Feb 1729	33
1483	WILKINS, Robert	John Taylor	Maryland	13 Jan 1726	17v
1484	WILKINSON, Stephen	Peter Simpson	Maryland	5 Dec 1726	28v
1485	WILKINSON, Thomas	John Taylor	Jamaica	14 Oct 1728	37v
1486	WILKS, Thomas	Neal MacNeal	Maryland	Feb 1727	49v
1487	WILLES, John	James Gerald	Jamaica	Feb 1727	49v
1488	WILLIAMS, Edward	John Taylor	Jamaica	2 Dec 1728	38
1489	WILLIAMS, Garrat	John Cooke	Virginia	13 Jan 1726	18v
1490	WILLIAMS, George	John Ball	Jamaica	26 Feb 1729	33
1491	WILLIAMS, John	John Cooke	Maryland	22 Feb 1726	19
1492	WILLIAMS, John	John Ball	Pennsylvania	16 Oct 1727	30v
1493	WILLIAMS, John	John Ball	Maryland	14 Oct 1728	37
1494	WILLIAMS, John	John Taylor	Jamaica	14 Oct 1728	37v
1495	WILLIAMS, John	Joseph Whilton	PENNSYLVANIA	15 Jan 1729	32
1496	WILLIAMS, John	William Burge	Antigua	13 Oct 1729	41v
1497	WILLIAMS, Joseph	William Burge	ANTIGUA	13 Oct 1729	42
1498	WILLIAMS, Mary	Samuel Gloynes	Jamaica	16 Oct 1727	31
1499	WILLIAMS, Rice	John Dykes	Pennsylvania	25 Aug 1725	21
1500	WILLIAMS, Richard	Jonathan Forward	Virginia	Dec 1732	62

1501	WILLIAMS, Thomas	John Taylor	Jamaica	18 Apr 1726	26
1502	WILLIAMS, Thomas	John Cooke	Jamaica	9 Aug 1726	26v
1503	WILLIAMS, Thomas	Peter Simpson	Maryland	5 Dec 1726	28v
1504	WILLIAMS, Thomas	Neal MacNeal	Pennsylvania	Feb 1733	59
1505	WILLIAMSON, John	Peter Simpson	Virginia	14 Oct 1728	37
1506	WILLIS, Samuel	James Gerald	Maryland	13 Jan 1726	19
1507	WILLIS, Thomas	James Gerald	Maryland	28 Feb 1727	25
1508	WILLOX, William	John Taylor	Jamaica	Jan 1731	53
1509	WILLS, John Jnr	Joseph Whilton	Jamaica	14 Apr 1729	40
1510	WILMOT, Edward	John Taylor	Maryland	5 Dec 1726	28v
1511	WILSON, Thomas	John Taylor	Jamaica	Jan 1731	53
1512	WIMPEY, Robert	Samuel Gloynes	Virginia	4 Dec 1727	32
1513	WISE, James	Richard Bateman	JAMAICA	18 Apr 1726	26
1514	WOOD, Abraham	John Taylor	Maryland	10 Oct 1726	27v
1515	WOOD, Francis	John Taylor	Jamaica	10 Oct 1726	27
1516	WOOD, William	James Gerald	Maryland	11 Jan 1728	29v
1517	WOODBRIDGE, John	Peter Simpson	Jamaica	Jan 1731	53
1518	WOODBURNE, John	John Cooke	Virginia	13 Jan 1726	18v
1519	WOODWARD, Joseph	John Taylor	Jamaica	2 Dec 1728	38
1520	WOODYER, James	James Gerald	Pennsylvania	Feb 1733	58v
1521	WOOLASTON, William	Neal MacNeal	Maryland	Dec 1732	61v
1522	WOOLLEY, James	Neal MacNeal	Pennsylvania	29 Apr 1728	33v
1523	WOOLMINTON, Roger	James Gerald	Jamaica	6 Dec 1725	24
1524	WORRALL, Mary	Neal MacNeal	Jamaica	Jul 1732	60
1525	WORTH, Ralph	John Cooke	Pennsylvania	18 Apr 1726	25v
1526	WRENN, Francis	James Gerald	Jamaica	6 Dec 1725	24
1527	WRIGHT, Andrew	Samuel Gloynes	Pennsylvania	18 Apr 1726	26
1528	WRIGHT, John	John Cooke	Virginia	10 Oct 1726	28
1529	WRIGHT, John	James Gerald	Maryland	Nov 1732	61
1530	WRIGHT, Samuel	John Cooke	Pennsylvania	18 Apr 1726	25v
1531	WRIGHT, Thomas	James Gerald	BARBADOS	15 Jan 1724	14

1532	WRIGHT, William	James Gerald	Jamaica	5 Apr 1725	20
1533	WRIGHT, William	William Cash	Antigua	26 Aug 1728	35v
1534	WRIN, William	William Cash	Jamaica	14 Jan 1730	39v
1535	WYBROW, John	John Dykes	Maryland	May 1720	5v

Y

1536	YATES, Henry	Bartholomew Voakes	N.D.	25 Aug 1725	20v
1537	YAXLEY, Robert	Peter Simpson	Pennsylvania	16 Oct 1727	31
1538	YEATES, George	James Gerald	Maryland	4 Dec 1727	32
1539	YEATES, Joseph	John Cooke	Maryland	22 Feb 1726	19
1540	YOUNG, Edward	James Gerald	Jamaica	6 Dec 1725	23v
1541	YOUNG, Isaac	John Cooke	MARYLAND	12 Jan 1727	25
1542	YOUNG, Mary	Peter Simpson	Maryland	18 Apr 1726	26
1543	YOUNG, Robert	William Cash	Maryland	14 Feb 1730	40
1544	YOUNGER, Susanna	Samuel Gloynes	Jamaica	16 Oct 1727	31